England
for the
English

England for the English

Richard Body

"There is a forgotten, nay almost forbidden word, which means more to me than any other. That word is England."

Sir Winston Churchill

NEW EUROPEAN PUBLICATIONS LONDON

Published in the United Kingdom in 2001 by

New European Publications Limited
14-16 Carroun Road
London SW8 1JT, England

Cover and page design Lloyd Allen
Copy setting Margaret Allen
Editing and proof reading   Maurice Temple Smith

British Library Cataloguing in Publication Data

ISBN 1872410-14-6

Composed in Elegant Garamond
Printed and bound in Great Britain by Biddles Ltd, Guildford.

To Marion,
part Scottish, part Swedish
and wholly English.

By the same author

Destiny or Delusion
(with Douglas Evans and others)
Victor Gollancs, 1971

Freedom and Stability in the Western World
(with Douglas Evans and others)
Barnes and Noble, 1975

Agriculture: the Triumph and the Shame
Maurice Temple Smith, 1982

Farming in the Clouds
Maurice Temple Smith, 1984

Red or Green for Farmers
Broad Leys, 1987

Europe of Many Circles
New European Publications, 1990

Our Food, Our Land
Random House, 1991

Breakdown of Europe
New European Publications, 1998

Contents

Introduction

"We're going to kill you", he said. The Commons had sat later than usual and I was sitting alone in the railway carriage in the early hours of the morning when the three young men confronted me. This was to be my second mugging. On the first occasion I lost ninety per cent of my eyesight and since I had no wish to lose the rest of it, I made no resistance as the ringleader rifled through my pockets.

Only a few days previously, a publisher had asked me to write this book and I had been reflecting on who were the English. As the man extracted such money as I had, it seemed to me this was an opportunity not to be missed. "Now I would be very grateful if you would help me over my book," I began. Taken aback by this strange affability, one by one they responded to my persistence and sat down on the opposite seats. Asking people at the bottom of the pile for a serious opinion is a form of flattery that works wonders. Half-an-hour later the conversation verged on the philosophical.

The three young men were black (my first muggers had been white). Failures at school, they had left unable to read or write and had done no work since - "racial discrimination, man." So they lived on social security - "it's nothing, man." They were loth to admit they dabbled in drugs, but it was obvious they did. Their parents were Christians but they themselves had become Moslems - "black man's religion, man." All white people treated them with contempt and they returned it

1

with hatred. "White people stole our country," and it seemed that simple logic gave them the right to steal from the white people. Unemployable and alienated in the land of their birth and now in their early twenties, what would their future life be in the next half-century?

Any notion of being British was decisively not for them – "We never British, man." But the thought that they could be English intrigued them. Unless those three, and a few million others of different racial origins, feel they belong to England and she to them, how can England be at ease with herself? And I do not mean Britain. I mean England, an England that is part of a United Kingdom which is set to become constitutionally very different.

There is a very good reason why Englishness cannot be a matter of race: the English are a multiracial people. Whether there is anyone of pure Anglo-Saxon descent is extremely doubtful, and if anyone who claims he is were to be DNA tested he might be surprised at the mixture of blood in his veins. Historians of the Anglo-Saxon period now agree that not all the British fled to the Celtic regions; many remained, some enslaved and others as freemen, and they or their descendants undoubtedly intermarried with the newcomers. We also know that a number of Romans, and some of black African origin, remained after the evacuation while others had married British wives. Quite apart from the Danes, Jutes, Vikings and Normans, after the Conquest French, Germans, Dutch, Russians, Spanish and Jewish were not alone among the tens of thousands who emigrated, coming especially to London and the larger cities. If anyone could compile a vast family tree embracing all his ancestors going back six or seven centuries, to the time when England's population was less than 3 millions, one might well find a regal forebear, certainly plenty of blue blood, as well as serfs and *émigrés*. Some years ago a constituent recently from India, who looked and spoke very much like an Indian, came to see me, wanting a house for himself and his family. Going through the bundle of faded documents that he produced, it seemed he was, through the Bowes-Lyon family, a seventh or eighth - perhaps ninth - cousin of the Queen. This, he insisted, was surely enough for me to persuade Her Majesty to allow him some accommodation in one of her properties. Having spent two years in India and learnt something of its customs, I explained that if he had had a similar relationship with a maharajah, no doubt somewhere suitable would have been found by his cousin, but over here we have a different view of cousinhood. Another fact to remember is that in the seventeenth and eighteenth centuries thousands of slaves from Africa and the West Indies came as domestic servants and status symbols - and following the custom in the plantations they took the names of their masters. It caused genealogists among the Victoria nouveaux riches to be seriously deluded about their ancestors. Even in the first half of the twentieth century a High Sheriff and his wife, both with skins of a hue as pure as the driven snow, brought into the world a black baby, which set the tongues a-wagging throughout their county, and ended their marriage in divorce. So, who knows how many of the English now have a few genes from Africa? When Matthew Parris calls his fellow-countrymen a race of mongrels he is not far wrong.

Nevertheless, the English are a distinct nation. To define them we can turn to international law. In determining the legal status of someone it draws a distinction between nationality, residence and domicile. We all begin life with a domicile of origin, which is the domicile of our parents. This remains our domicile until there is clear evidence that it changes to a domicile of choice. By going to live in another country one changes one's residence but not necessarily one's domicile; indeed acquiring a new nationality does not necessarily imply a new domicile, for one can enjoy dual nationality. The test is whether one wishes to settle in another country; essentially it is the country in which one feels most at home. It implies that one has turned one's back upon the country of one's origin. Lord Tebbit's cricket test – which team do you cheer, the one from the country of your birth or the one belonging to the country to which you have emigrated? – has been much maligned, but an international lawyer would probably say that it more or less hits the target. The authoritative *Private International Law* by Cheshire and Fifoot[1] lists five principles about domicile, which have a bearing upon the thesis of this book. Everyone has a domicile but no one can have two. Domicile signifies a connection with a single system of territorial law, and if someone moves to a new country he is still presumed to be domiciled in his old country until he himself decides to settle permanently in the new one. Finally, English law determines the domicile of who is English in the courts of England. Thus a Scotsman , for example, may reside in England for many years and have a British nationality, but is still domiciled in Scotland until it is clear he feels more at home in England in the sense that England has become his country. So when he celebrates England defeating his native country at Wembley he has almost certainly acquired a domicile of choice.

What is clear is that someone who happens to reside in England, no matter the length of time or whether he or she brings up a family in England, has not become English unless they are content to accept the core values and beliefs of the country. "Culture" has become something of a Humpty Dumpty word and can be heard every day with a variety of meanings. However, it is gratifying to find how it is defined in Chambers Twenty First Century Dictionary, a work which oozes political correctness (it even has an entry for "Significant Other"). Culture is given two meanings and the primary one is "the customs, ideas, values etc., of a particular civilisation, society or social group, especially at a particular time". So when the father climbs up the steps to the National Gallery urging his doubting children to "have a bit of culture", he is using the word in the secondary sense, the appreciation of art, music etc. The Germans with their *Kultur* use the word mainly in the primary sense. So did the Victorians; had Gladstone or Disraeli been told that one day there would sit at the Cabinet table a Secretary of State for Culture, they would have wondered what on earth he had to do.

[1] Cheshire and Fifoot, *Private International Law*; OUP, 1992.

Introduction

Students of Anglo-Saxon history will claim that there are certain parts of the culture of those early times which are with England still. That they have survived at all says something about their durability and the influence they must have had in the evolution of England's history. Those Angles and Saxons as well as the Jutes who migrated to southern Britain came to settle and farm not in tribal communities, but as individuals, owning their own land. Their quest for individual freedom naturally begot toleration towards what others said or did. By the time King Alfred united the kingdoms they were ready to embrace a unique conception of the rule of law and to live by a code born of their own experiences, putting them at variance both with the ways of the Continent and with those of the Celtic peoples. That difference persists and those facts about the origins of the English still lie at the very roots of Englishness, its core values and beliefs.

It is those values and beliefs that await anyone who now comes to live in England, and this can raise problems. Anyone coming to live in another country is either willing or unwilling to accept its culture. If willing, they deserve to be welcomed; and if they wish to settle permanently and be assimilated, they ought to have all the rights and responsibilities of those already settled here. If they are unwilling, the English sense of toleration will permit them to have feelings of hatred or contempt and even, within liberal bounds, to express them. However the multiculturist wants to go further. His moral relativism extends to what people do as well as think and say. About their actions and their behaviour to others, the multiculturist tells us to be non-judgmental. No doubt an immigrant's culture may be as good as, perhaps even better than England's. But that is scarcely the point, for any civil society, in the true sense of the word, has to have an accepted ethos to bind its members together, as a later chapter shows.

Those who are English because of their domicile of origin ought to have a mindset that broadly accepts those core values, acquiring them by instinct, upbringing, education or, most likely, all the many influences of the civil society in which they live. And those who have come to England acquiring a domicile of choice, and therefore becoming English, ought to acquire a similar mindset.

Sadly one uses the words "ought" and "should". One is forced to do so because many thousands of pupils have left our schools denied that mindset, and their parents, despite their domicile, have, in the name of political correctness, had barriers placed in the way to acquiring a knowledge of how their homeland has evolved. A later chapter tells how this is happening, looks at its dangers, and queries the motives of those responsible.

A discussion about any nation makes it necessary to draw a distinction between multiracialism and multiculturalism. Too often the two are spoken in the same breath as logically inseparable, and indeed as interchangeable terms. If culture is about going to the cinema, reading a book or making that difficult decision whether to choose a tandoori or fish and chips, it matters not a jot how multicultural we are. The greater the mix, the wider is the freedom of choice. The *Guardian* writers who go on so much about multiculturalism are more likely to be exercised about choosing between *Tosca* and *Swan Lake*, or whether to dine on the Italian fare in Soho or in the nice little Spanish restaurant just opened up in Islington. All this is about culture in the secondary sense; and even before Alfred's reign the Saxons are known to have traded as far afield as the Levant, returning with different foods, jewellery and other things to give their fellow countrymen a wider selection to choose from. Not then, nor at any time, have the people of England been chauvinistic in their cultural tastes. In fact, they have been as eclectic as any nation.

But is that the sense in which advocates of multiculturalism use the word? If so, there is no argument, and no need to raise the subject – as if the English had to be persuaded, when they have been convinced for fifteen centuries. No, it is plain that they are engaged in the vice of obfuscating. Trying to persuade people about a word with two meanings is fertile ground for obfuscation. You speak as if you mean A, which is generally agreed, when you really mean B; and if you continue to do so for long enough, your listeners will believe both A and B are equally desirable. It is dishonest, and also very dangerous.

Culture (in the primary sense, of course) is the bond that binds together a civil society. Removing the bond is like extracting the cement from a wall: give the wall a push and the edifice collapses. The collapse can perhaps be averted if the wall has a number of other supports. So, too, with a civil society. Take away its culture and it will disintegrate into being just a mass of nihilistic people. But some sort of cohesion can be kept with artificial supports in the form of an increasing number of laws and regulations, with ever more bureaucrats and quangos. However those measures will work only in the short term.

The writers, broadcasters, politicians and academics - in all quite a legion - who espouse multiculturalism either have not thought through the meaning of culture or they have failed to grasp the essence of a civil society. Once a civil society - a group of people no matter how large - loses its distinctive values and beliefs, it also loses its social cohesion: in a word it becomes de-civilised. A de-civilised society is a revolutionary's dream and among the cultured pundits may well be some covert revolutionaries yearning to mount barricades. It must be said that the far Left groups are extremely active in stirring up racial hatred among Asians and black people, and have led the accusations against the police, the army and other institutions.

Because the roots of England's culture lie in the reasons why the English sought asylum in Britain, their culture is not one that they wholly share with the Celts. That made the United Kingdom to a degree multiculturalist, but the clash of values was overlaid by a sense of unity with the coming of the British Empire, and four nations shared in the pride and glory it evoked. All four were content to be British. With the demise of the Empire eyes were turned to Europe. But centrifugal forces, similar to those that dissolved the Empire, will have an impact upon the European Union, as they are having today upon the United Kingdom.

Then is England to be on her own? Why not? No, not an island of little Englanders, on the contrary. Nor need the prospect rouse fear, anxiety or shame. No, England can have a future greater than her past.

So do the following pages invite a dormant nationalism? No, not nationalism, neither chauvinism nor jingoism, nor xenophobia. Nationalism is always assertive and therefore directed against others; chauvinism is a prejudice, and jingoism merely boastfulness. Xenophobia, like all phobias, is a fear. There is another word - patriotism.

"I love my homeland," said an Italian, "because I love all homelands." They are the words of a true patriot. Patriotism, of course, means no more and no less than love of one's own homeland. England is as she is because that is what, for fifteen centuries, the English have made her. In their making she has become different from other homelands; and the essential differences have come about because of a different culture. That is so even with the landscape. Visitors to parts of the English-speaking world where the climate is not dissimilar, in Virginia, British Columbia, Tasmania and New Zealand especially, are amazed at places where the scenery is so like parts of England, and to learn that is how the early settlers made them in the image of the land they left behind. As they walk down streets in Hobart or Christchurch, they will find a built environment no different from what might be found in England.

But for a few mountains, the English countryside has been transformed over many centuries by the people who have lived there, according to how they wished it to be. It is the visible evidence of their values and beliefs. So, too, with the artefacts of the built environment; as John Ruskin put it, they are the products of contemporary culture. The intangible feature of any country - its laws, ethics and all else that add up to a distinctive way of doing things - more obviously stem from a nation's mindset, that particular bundle of values and beliefs special to itself.

Patriotism being the love of a homeland can be seen as an extension of a fondness for one's own home as well as the town, village or county in which one is settled. Affection for our own home requires no hatred for the one next door - simply we do not move in when it falls vacant. But no matter how much we like living where we do - in house, town or village or county - we can be sure there is something to be done to make it more loveable. Patriotism therefore is not blind to what is wrong.

Just as we want to put right what is wrong with our home (that is, if we love it and wish to remain there), so the patriot feels the same about his homeland. That makes him a public servant. And, we might ask those who sneer at him, what is wrong with that?

The current distrust of patriotism and of Englishness is one indication of how the English today face a crisis in the history of their culture. If they are to survive that crisis they must decide how their country is to relate to the rest of the British Isles, to Europe and to the world. That decision is what this book is about.

Chapter 1
The Revenge of Culture

In the second half of the twentieth century the number of self-governing nations eligible to join the United Nations nearly quadrupled. Although many were the erstwhile colonies or protectorates of European powers, most of them were new states breaking away from larger ones. Europe has seen the division of Czechoslovakia, the disruption of Yugoslavia, the rebirth of the Baltic states and the dissolution of the Soviet Union. Within the European Union it is not just the Basques who want to break away; in Italy an industrious North has shown by its votes; that its people wish to be shot of what they see as an indolent South. The Bretons and Savoyans are raising the call for independence, and even in little Belgium the union of two nations is demonstrably ill at ease. Elsewhere in the world at any one time there are several armed conflicts raging, each a civil war, and generally they have ended only when another new state has been created. Although these wars have been increasing ever since the Second World War, it is a notable fact that wars between independent nation states have been extremely rare, which seems to rebut the long-held view that by nature they are a threat to peace.

Not all these new states are born of a civil war; in many cases the insurgence is more peaceful although the leaders may suffer the fate of political prisoners. Amnesty International has reported that there are sixty countries with political prisoners, which is one indication of more new states to come. Mr Daniel Moynihan, on behalf of the United States, has warned the

United Nations that another fifty members would be eligible to join in the next fifty years, all probably as the result of a civil war.

Why should this be happening? It contradicts an interpretation of history which prevailed throughout most of the twentieth century. Ultimately, it is said, there will be a world government - one human race living in one political, economic and cultural unit - and we are inexorably moving towards that end. Hence (so we are told) the need to merge nation states into regional unions, which in turn will join neighbours to form mega-states embracing whole continents before reaching the final stage of one government for all humanity. Nationalists, racialists and xenophobes and their ilk will stand in the way; their silly arguments will be brushed aside once the people understand that nation states are the root of all evil between nations. Convincing them of this will be a noble mission for those who go out from the universities to teach history.

But culture is having its revenge. To fuse different cultures into one goes against the grain of human nature. The attempt must of necessity demand compromises to be made. And why should a people with long established values and beliefs be called upon to value and believe differently?

Empire builders, though, can be more successful. They have merged cultures in other ways, for they had the power to do so. Power given is power to be used, whether in the hands of a traffic warden or an emperor; and in the case of the latter, it will be exercised even by the lowest ranks in the imperial hierarchy. No need, they may think, to explain or reach a compromise. They are the superior people, since they are the conquerors, and since the conquered are inferior their culture must be too. There may be a flaw in the their reasoning; it does not matter; their power can ride over any logical niceties. Most of the large nation states were themselves empires. One more powerful country would by military force, by a treaty under duress or even by inter-marriage, incorporate a lesser one, and often then proceeded to embrace others.

Germany, as such a union, has survived since Bismarck because, although the kingdoms, principalities and dukedoms that comprised it had some cultural differences, they also had a very large degree of cultural homogeneity, and this has served to cement the union. That could scarcely be said of the Austro-Hungarian Empire or the Russian Empire that became the Soviet Union, nor the merger by the more peaceful means which united the Slovakians with the Czechs. In the Indian sub-continent East Pakistan felt herself to be a dependency of West Pakistan, while broke away to form Bangladesh while Sikhs and Kashmiris, feeling no part of India, are resisting rule from Delhi.

Within the United Kingdom the pursuit of a cultural identity, buttressed by self-government, is in the minds of an ever-increasing number in the Celtic countries. The English mind fails to understand what has happened in countless families in Scotland and Wales, as it has in Ireland. These Celtic families are an influential minority who have been proud of their inheritance and have handed down from one generation to another the legends of the past. In Wales they are about how the last Welsh Prince of Wales was slaughtered by an Englishman (unhappily with the same surname as this author), about how their language and literature were suppressed and their common lands expropriated, along with other tales to keep alive sentiments of oppression. In Scotland stories of the Clearances or of the migration to Nova Scotia lack nothing in their vividness. Nor will the Battle of Culloden or the butchery by Cumberland be overlooked as father retells these legends to his children, who will retell them again in their turn. *Braveheart* confirmed it all, and helps to give the legends another lease of life. The English, having themselves no call to harbour such grievances, will only begin to grasp the effect of this tradition, going back many generations, when they hear at first hand how latent is the wish for revenge, and how it has lain within these Celtic hearts for so long. These families may not be a majority in the southern counties of Wales and in most of the Scottish Lowlands where the tradition will have died long ago, but in other parts of both countries it has given passion to the nationalist cause. It is these same people who rather like the notion of a European Union which gives them money (mainly from the English and Germans) and whose officials have drawn up a map on which every country in the European Union is marked, except England. They see it as a mechanism to make them viable countries freed from their oppressive neighbour.

In *Global Paradox*, John Naisbitt has shown that the more the people of the world become enfolded in one integrated economy - a single global market place - the more they will react by striving for cultural independence. Whenever different peoples, each one culturally homogeneous, are yoked together, a centrifugal force will be at work; and Naisbitt predicts it will be wholly practical for each one to form its own nation state. As about a thousand can be identified, the potential for as many new self-governing entities is vast. With all tariffs and other barriers to trade removed, even the smallest of them will enjoy a viable economy, as viable as Rutland is within an economically integrated Britain. How the UN will manage its affairs with this membership is another matter.

The dangers of the culture clashes in the global economy have been highlighted by Benjamin Barber in his equally readable *Jihad v McWorld*. Jihad betokens the struggle for a faith, a zeal to protect a culture; McWorld represents universal McDonalds, Coca Colas and the rest of the output that homogenises the world's commerce. One might imagine that Jihad's zeal, having created another state to protect its culture, would erect barriers against the alien goods, but this may not be the case. The Serbian sniper is seen to swallow his Coca Cola before taking aim at the Bosnian for much the same reason as the Eurosceptic may buy a Mercedes. Cultural assertiveness does not require commercial chauvinism. Nor does the goal of self-determination imply an autarkic regime, for in this new world we pick and choose, we have the tangible goods we like from home or abroad, and we choose the intangible moral and political ones too. We come back to the two meanings of culture: a nation can be both monocultural and multicultural, provided the former is in the primary sense and the latter in the secondary. In that way Jihad and McWorld can live in peace.

Now the Jihad's genie has popped out of the nationalists' bottle in three of the countries of Britain. As for the fourth, two events at the close of the twentieth century should persuade the English that the wraith is here to stay, continuing to dance before their eyes. Until 1998 few people in England had contemplated that the United Kingdom was in danger of being dissolved. Once devolution was on the way with a Scottish Parliament, the upsurge in support for the Scottish Nationalist Party became inevitable; and the opinion polls show that at some time in the future the Scottish Parliament will have a majority large enough to lead to the repeal of the Act of Union. Whether that parliamentary majority is elected soon or a decade or two later is beside the point. Who can believe with certainty that by the year 2020 the United Kingdom will still be intact? It means that in the intervening years its second largest country is no more than a temporary member of the Union. As another chapter shows, after Scotland joined the Union, she had a major advantage in being British, for she could join in the building of a great empire, which provided prosperity at home and opportunities for her sons abroad. It is not unnatural for them now to wonder whether there is any advantage in compromising their own culture by asserting their Britishness.

The second event was the election of the Northern Ireland Assembly. The Unionists may have won, but not by the massive majorities they used to have in the House of Commons or at Stormont. West Belfast then elected a Unionist, so did the city of Londonderry and the southern halves of Counties Down and Armagh. In those days no Sinn Fein voice was heard in Queen's University where the Union Jack was raised without dissent. Since then a steady trickle of its talented graduates from Unionist families has crossed the Channel to seek a more secure career, leaving behind the nationalist-minded to take the posts that would have been theirs. Some tens of thousands of other young men and women have also come over to England or Scotland, while others have joined their kindred in Canada, New Zealand or Australia. This factor in itself is eventually going to place the Unionists in a minority, but so long as Protestants and Roman Catholics differ about birth control, the decline in the former's majority must accelerate. What, then, is the prospect for Ulster in, say, the year 2020? That's two out of four countries edging towards an exit.

Whether the politicians elected to the Welsh Assembly will have their appetite whetted for more power will be known well before the year 2020, but the outcome cannot lessen the certainty that the United Kingdom of Great Britain and Northern Ireland cannot be sustained.

Those of us who have believed in the Union may react in a number of ways as we come to realise what its demise will mean. We can wring our hands in despair, although once it is a *fait accompli* that would be rather futile. We can say good riddance and curse our former partners for their infidelity, but that will only make matters worse, as marriage counsellors warn divorcing couples. Today we are often urged to think positively about our setbacks and misfortunes, to turn them to our advantage, and the subsequent chapters set out how that may be done. Over the centuries the English have shown themselves to be a pragmatic people and at times of adversity to be able to adapt to its outcome. Once the dissolution comes, those qualities are the very ones to be brought into play and, to see the English yet again finding another role and a new status in the world. In the meanwhile we can put England's dilemma in its historic perspective. As a unitary state, the United Kingdom can lay no claim to antiquity. In its present form it is a creature of the twentieth century; its zenith was reached only a generation before that; and less than two centuries previously only England and Wales were united. In England's life of one and a half millennia, she has been constitutionally independent of the other three countries for nearly two-thirds of the time.

The genie having popped out of the Scottish, Welsh and Irish bottles, we might ask ourselves whether some English genie is poised to leap and tease. One small symptom is that hoteliers report that residents sign a register as English ten times more frequently than they did a few years ago. More important is the "West Lothian question". If English MPs are no longer allowed to vote on Scottish affairs, why should Scottish MPs be allowed to vote on English affairs? This question is now heard on English lips more indignantly and less elegantly than ever it was originally put by Tam Dalyell. The letter pages of any of our national newspapers also bear witness to the rumblings. The House of Commons has seventy representatives from Scotland. Their votes are of equal value to those of any English Member and they have their say in what the English should have and what they should do. Seventy is a substantial proportion of the total membership and a still greater one of the Parliamentary Labour Party. A future Labour government with a smaller majority may depend upon it to get its business through the House. The West Lothian Question will then blow across England rising to the fury of a gale force 8. How will anyone be able to answer a simple point: why should the English tolerate being told which laws they are to obey and what taxes they are to pay and how their money should be spent by seventy men and women they do not elect and over whom they have no control, and who above all, have a prior obligation to protect the interests of people in another country?

Now that Wales and Northern Ireland have their assemblies, the English are the only people in the United Kingdom who have no representative body of their own. They are in the position of the parent whose teenage daughter defines her position on family property as "What's mine is mine and what's yours belongs to the family".

If this obvious injustice is not put right there is a real danger of an English backlash whose demands may go well beyond the modest reform that would satisfy them now. As it is, it would not even need any new legislation to correct this constitutional anomaly. A resolution in the House of Commons would be enough to ensure that only English MPs voted on affairs that affected only the English, and a basic principle of representative democracy would be restored.

Most people in England now know about the imbalance of public expenditure between their country and the other three. (£144 per head for the Scots to every £100 per head for the English, so it is frequently said.) It came home to me when I met three young people in my constituency; none of them could conceivably be dismissed as little Englanders: they had travelled around Europe, one was at university in Madrid, and one planned to work overseas. Far from being xenophobic, they seemed typical of a generation which enjoyed their visits to the Continent and with friends abroad. They began to speak of England. I queried this, suggesting they meant Britain. A robust response persuaded me that the English genie will at any moment pop out of the bottle too. For the purpose of this book I have spoken to scores of people of varying ages, occupations and outlooks, and in all regions of England, and I have included Asians and West Indians who have settled here. From them I have heard nothing to dispel the fear that there is an awakening of national consciousness. Inevitably it takes many different forms and one must not generalise too much. Nonetheless a few solid points emerge. Of the many I have asked whether they think themselves British or English, the number who reply "English" is a growing majority. They have also been the most decisive in their reply. Five years ago most of them would have said the opposite. What has been striking is the number who are of Welsh, Scottish or Irish origin who now speak of themselves as English. The Asians and West Indians demurred at calling themselves English and were not often happier at being British. When given the legal definition of English they almost all expressed a willingness to accept the description and some added that they would be proud to be English (the Commission for Race Relations, please note).

Far from being weakened economically by the disintegration of the United Kingdom, England would enjoy some measurable gains. The six million Scots receive £20,000 millions from the Treasury. This enables them to have better schools, hospitals, roads and policing then England; and any visitors from England keeping their eyes open can see the difference. The transfer of this massive amount of wealth has been going for many years and so far there is no indication that it may be reduced. It represents an average of £12 a week for the average family. Restored to the English, an increase in purchasing power could be translated into a few hundred thousand new jobs. Alternatively, the Chancellor of the Exchequer could have enough revenue to spare to tell the Secretary of State for Health that he could build twenty more hospitals every year.

Northern Ireland and Wales together cost England rather less than Scotland. The former is a special case and so long as she remains in the Union one hopes the English will not resent spending so much on the consequences of terrorism. When eventually the Nationalists outnumber the Unionists and a Dublin government takes over, there will be a further net gain to London's Treasury, which can only mean another increase in the purchasing power of the English. A majority of the Welsh may never assert the right to self-determination, yet if that day came, they would relieve the English taxpayer of another burden. It might be modest compared with that imposed by the Scots and Irish, but even if it represented only half a penny off the standard rate of income tax, it could give the English face at least half a smile.

Already there is evidence that the Scots are beginning to realise that they do rather well out of the fiscal system. The failure of the Scottish Nationalists to win a majority in the new Parliament suggests that the Scots see the advantage of being semi-detached. The Labour party with or without a coalition partner may stay in power for many years, but sooner or later the cry "time for a change" will be heard, and the leading opposition party will take the reins. The Scottish Nationalists would then proceed to their ultimate goal and the reason for their existence.

Now, that being at least several years away, let us consider how the English will react in the meanwhile. Only an extraordinary degree of naivety can persuade anyone that they will overlook what is happening and how it affects them personally, their pockets, their standard of living and their sense of country. First of all, the English will see the Scots making their own laws, and in a host of ways they are likely to be different from those in England. If considered more sensible or more appropriate for the times, these changes will not go unnoticed south of the Border. Perhaps just a little envy may creep into the minds of the English. Visitors who cross the Border will observe the better schools, hospitals, roads and policing and will be more readily telling their friends and neighbours of what is going on "up there". There is nothing like first-hand accounts by an eye witness who is a friend to persuade one of the truth. And the truth will hurt. "Up there you don't wait a year for hip replacements, they do it for you inside a month." "Driving on that new road to Inverness you get there in half the time, and we didn't get snarled up in a traffic jam." "In Glasgow it was amazing, plenty of policemen on the beat, and you could walk around the city quite safely at any time of the night." "You should see the new schools they are building - not like that rotten place our Joan goes to down here."

An endless stream of anecdotes will be heard, and envy and resentment will grow. Will the English be told nothing about the extra £20,000 millions they are paying for the Scots? This is the point when every MP elected south of the Border will have to raise his voice. To explain to a growing number of constituents, roused by the disparity in public services, why they must put up with what is worse, the MPs will tell the electorate the obvious truth, that they too can have schools, hospitals, roads, policing (and other things as well) as good as the Scots if they are willing to pay more in taxation; and the electorate will reply that they would rather have the £20,000 millions spent on themselves rather than the Scots.

Foreigners who have written about different periods of England's history have often commented upon how complacent the English have been about major political or social issues that in other countries would bring a people out into the streets, and how long-suffering the English are when misgoverned. These historians have also noted that there comes a time when the English can be aroused, and once roused there's steel in their hearts and a grim determination that drives them on to victory.

In the end, therefore, it may not be for the Scots to decide that they should retain the privileged position – in the true sense of the word – that they now enjoy to the manifest disadvantage of the English. They may be told that the semi-detached arrangement secured in 1999 no longer suits the English. To bring it to an end may prove to be quite simple. Notwithstanding the seventy Scottish votes in the House, a majority will cut off the largesse of £20,000 million because the English people will make it plain that their money is to be spent within their own country. This will not itself take Scotland out of the UK, but the effect upon the Scots will be obvious. The one cogent argument against the Scottish Nationalists will be washed away. The Scots will have little, possibly nothing, to lose by returning a Nationalist government and voting in the subsequent referendum as their new government will urge them to do.

There is also a fundamental reason why the English and Scots will part company. Their respective cultures have grown from different roots. As it is culture more than race that is dissolving the unions of nations in every continent of the world, we need not be surprised at the dissolution or at a constitutional transformation with like effect taking place in a union of the four nations of the British Isles. It is time to realise the significance of a single truth: how a nation is to be governed is ultimately determined by its culture (in the primary sense, of course). Any attempt to govern according to another culture will fail eventually. So if the cultures of two nations are materially different, their union is doomed to be a scene of conflict. That is culture's revenge.

Chapter 2

As It Was in the Beginning, is Now

The books of potted history, especially the ones used in schools, are less than fair in describing the Angles, Saxons and Jutes who came to settle in Albion. Upon generations of pupils a wrong impression has been left about why their distant forbears turned their backs upon the Continent to make England a different country in which to live. It is true, though, that before they came, both during the latter part of the Roman occupation and afterwards more frequently, corsairs from across the North Sea landed upon the beaches on the eastern seaboard. These buccaneers disembarked to ravage and pillage and, having gained their spoils, sailed back to the ports from whence they came. They were of seafaring families, whose other sons went fishing or trading among the ports of northern Europe. Many years later, after the Anglo-Saxon settlement had begun, some of their descendants took over the ports on the southern coast and from them set sail to Iberia, the Mediterranean and even the Levant as traders and no doubt as freebooters too. A century or two later, when King Alfred resolved to establish a maritime defence, it would have been men from these families who founded the Royal Navy. From the outset they created for the English a reputation as a great seafaring nation, but they did not create England herself.

Returning to their homeland, the original buccaneers would have told of their adventures, and the stories would have been retold many times as news of a country vacated by the Romans passed into the hinterland far from the sea. It was here on the plains of northern Europe that Angles, Saxons and Jutes – the country cousins of the buccaneers – were striving to earn a livelihood in conditions that offered no prospect of peace. No farmer begins to sow his seeds in the spring and nurtures the crop through the summer months unless there is hope for a harvest to repay his labour. But their homeland had become no place for honest husbandry. Tactitus had already described in vivid terms how they often laboured in vain, but now the whole region was in turmoil. With the Roman Empire disintegrating, there was no protection against the hordes surging through their lands from the east. In the first half of 400 AD, Attila the Hun, with a train of thousands in his wake, laid waste the land wherever they chose to go, thieving, raping and terrorising any who stood in their way. Of Attila it was said, "where his horses trod, the grass would never grow." The Franks, Magyars and Mongols, too descended upon the plains of northern Europe, and were no more merciful as they ransacked and robbed their way across them. Without protection against these hordes, there could be no hope of a harvest safely gathered in, nor could anyone see the prospect of a benign empire to take the place of Caesar's to stand guard over their lands in the future. The only hope, it must have seemed to them, was in the fertile land they had heard tell about far away across a sea they had never seen. Moreover, it was an island, they understood, severed by a great sea from a continent now cursed with invaders lawless and ruthless.

So with grim determination they set off on a terrible journey to be England's first asylum seekers. How terrible it was is difficult to imagine. We know they went in flat-bottomed boats, wide enough to carry the possessions they would need, such as axes and ploughs as well as a few livestock like hens and pigs, perhaps a sheep or two, but nothing so large as a cow or horse; and there had to be room for the womenfolk and children as well as food and water. With no keel or sails, they crossed the sea as fast as the men could row; and it was this that must have made the journey so terrible. The boats were broad and heavy laden and they rowed against a wind from the west. We do not know how many men were at the oars, but the legendary tales speak of each boat taking many weeks to make the journey, so we can visualise a boat drifting back with the wind when oars were rested, and how through the night the men must have struggled. As to whether the food and water lasted for all those weeks, again we do not know for certain, nor whether they had strength enough to feel any sense of triumph once they finally beached upon their haven. They had come with no intention of returning; this was to be their homeland and they had to set about getting food and shelter and to clear the ground for the seeds they had brought. The books of potted history found in the schools tell us nothing of this epic voyage or the privations endured; they do not even tell the reader that these founders of England were of a quite different ilk and inclination from those seafaring buccaneers they write about.

As those schoolbooks do little more than regurgitate what previous ones have described they have denied the reader the knowledge about the first English settlers which can now be distilled from archaeological discoveries in the twentieth century, modern translations of ancient manuscripts and rigorous scrutiny of legendary stories. Following the study of Anglo-Saxon language in the universities, today's student can take advantage of several works of more recent times, notably *The Anglo Saxons* by Sir Frank Stenton[1], or for the middle-brow there is *The Offshore Islanders* by the ever-readable Paul Johnson.[2]

For centuries the Celts of Cornwall and Wales have been taught that what is claimed to be England was once the home of their fathers. Of course, it is true that some tens of thousands of Celts had occupied southern Albion; but there were Roman soldiers and civilians too, and many of them stayed behind rather than make their way back to Italy, and no doubt among them were many who had intermarried and had children of mixed descent. What must be certain is that the early settlers

[1] Sir Frank Stenton, *The Anglo Saxons*; OUP, 1989.

[2] Paul Johnson, *The Offshore Islanders*; Weidenfeld & Nicolson, 1972.

came not to fight a war but to farm in peace. In all probability, the indigenous inhabitants along the coastal areas had already fled in the face of recurring raids by the sea-faring buccaneers.

Later waves of immigrants may have been of a more aggressive nature than the first settlers. It is incontrovertible that the Saxons in particular drove many of the Celts westwards, for they came to settle in Essex and Sussex and they also moved further into the hinterland than the Angles and the Jutes. Even in those areas, many of the Celts remained and it was not long before the two races intermarried. The Saxons wanted the lowlands where the soil was most fertile and the terrain amenable to the plough; the hills, it seems, were mostly left to the Celts. Accommodating them in this way may have been more an act of convenience than generosity, for it probably let the crop-growing Saxons taste some Celtic mutton at no cost to themselves. As further Saxons came over and the population increased, more land was needed and the demand for Celtic territory grew. If the Celts are to speak of their Diaspora or the Anglo-Saxon conquest, they ought to concede that it was a process that took many generations and that many of their kin stayed behind. The newcomers sought only arable land and when they reached the hills of the West Country and beyond the Severn, they went no further. The Celts were then as now stockmen or graziers, while the Saxons were men of the plough.

A song in *Oklahoma*, which is about the founding of a new state, tells us that one man can handle a cow and the other a plough, and there is not much friendship between them. So it was in the foundation of England. To this day agricultural economists speak of the livestock and arable sectors as tending to be in conflict, and farmers have for generations quoted the old adage "up corn, down horn" and vice versa, for when one prospers it is often at the expense of the other.

That the Anglo-Saxons were principally arable farmers, growers rather than graziers, is borne out by what we see even today in England. The eastern half of the country has tended to belong to the arable sector, while the western half, along with

Wales and Scotland, has been predominantly given over to live-stock. When arable farming went into decline with the intro-duction of cheaper grains, in particular wheat, from Australia and North America, thousands of farms that had grown arable crops for many centuries no longer provided a livelihood. Their owners or tenants, almost to a man, had Anglo-Saxon or Danish names; and in the first half of the twentieth century their holdings were taken over by thousands of Welshmen and Scotsmen, who put the fields down to grass and thus began a great dairy industry. Despite what is often said, the inter-war years were not a period of agricultural depression, because the decline in arable farming was accompanied by a massive expan-sion in the livestock sector. The villages of southern England bear witness: many a Hughes, a Davies or a Jones, or names from the lowlands of Scotland will be found, their grandfathers having taken over from Anglo-Saxon descendants who had neither the inclination nor the temperament to turn to another kind of agriculture.

The livestock farmer must decide matters of life and death, for those in his charge will sooner or later go to be butchered. He may not be a hard man, but sentimentalism is rationed. His arable neighbour can have and usually does have a different temperament. Do we possibly infer from this that the Anglo-Saxons recoiled from livestock farming out of a regard for other sentient beings? That might be going too far, but the evidence suggests that they showed a concern for the welfare of animals. Nor were they great meat-eaters like the Franks or the Celts. They could have had as many animals as would keep them in meat every day throughout the year; that they did not do so may possibly be because they and their wives and children drew back from the business of slaughtering the creatures they had cared for, fed and nursed in sickness. Later centuries are more revealing: the Anglo-Saxon's dog and his horse were looked after better than those of the Norman conquerors. Today the English compared to the Welsh, Scots or Irish, set up more animal charities, introduce more legislation on animal welfare and write more feelingly yet knowledgeably about their animals. Is this something new about the English or does it descend from long ago? If the former, what has caused it to burst forth out of nowhere? As it is difficult to think of a cause, perhaps it is part of the inheritance from long ago.

Although little is known about how the migration was organised, we can suppose that almost everyone who set off on the journey had a most limited knowledge of anything other than a simple life on the land. To think of them as peasants would be true, but they were of sterling qualities. Among them were men of strong leadership who were probably the chiefs in their homeland, and unquestionably they were acknowledged as such once they reached the shore of Britain. Legendary tales came to be told of these men; embellished maybe, but the stories of what they achieved have about them the ring of truth. Even before they boarded the boats, we can imagine debates taking place as to how they would live together and the rules they would agree upon; and later as sweat poured down from exhausted limbs upon the oars, a vision of another world would have danced across their minds.

From everything we know about them, we can be sure their motive for migration was to seek a land where they could farm and live (the two being much the same) in an environment safer than the one they left behind. Hence a system of land ownership had to be devised that was accepted as fair to all.

What could be fairer than each family being allocated enough land to keep itself? Deciding how to apply the principle was not so easy, for much depended upon the quality of the soil and how much timber there was for fuel. So no hard-and-fast acreage was laid down, but throughout the Saxon settlements the average seems to have ranged from about forty acres where the soil was good to about one hundred and eighty where it was poor. Such holdings – called hides – have survived within living memory. The common agricultural policy of the European Union works to the advantage of the larger farmer rather than his smaller neighbour. For if a farmer is given an artificially high price for what he produces, he will have an incentive to go on increasing production. As a smaller farmer is constrained by the size of his holding from raising its output, he is at a disadvantage compared with his competitor with a larger farm. Thus they gradually go out of business; holdings are amalgamated, and the number engaged in agriculture goes into decline. Nevertheless, the total number of people employed in food production remains the same, for the more a farm grows in size, the more it has to be supplied and serviced from outside. The man in Coventry making a tractor becomes part of food production as much as the man who drives it; and the man on the North Sea oil rig has a hand in getting fertiliser despatched to a farm hundreds of miles away.

Is that disgression a whimsical leap from what was happening fifteen centuries ago? No, it is the first example of how English culture is being changed. From Kent across to Dorset there used to be several thousand small farms, each one of them about forty acres. In Berkshire they were called "little bargains", and Mary Mitford in *Our Village*[1] wrote about the kind of people whose homes and livelihoods they were. Most of them in more recent years had a bit of everything: a few cows, a pig or two, geese and hens running around, a cart horse, an orchard and a garden with more vegetables than flowers. Beyond were fields in which they grew wheat and oats and other crops, while the other fields were pasture for the horse and the cows. The family was made self-sufficient in most things, and a weekly visit to the market to sell the surpluses usually, but not always, yielded enough to buy what else was needed. It may be too fanciful to think that any of those holdings of the first half of the twentieth century were the same as those marked out by the earliest Saxons, for farms have altered their shape, fields having constantly changed hands and farmhouses moved to places more convenient. Still, a feature of Englishness from long ago managed to survive for many centuries.

---

[1] Mary Mitford, *Our Village*; 5 volumes, Whittaker, Treacher & Co, 1830. Many shortened editions since published, by Macmillan & Co and others.

What is more, it remains an idyll for as many Englishmen as were ever able to put it into practice. To this day their instinct to grow things finds expression in gardens, allotments and the humble window-box. Only in England, not even in Wales or Scotland, are there so many miles of suburban houses that can be seen, each with a garden which is tended with care and pride. Only in England are gardens open to the public on such a scale; and in the summer months they welcome many millions of the English. Some gardens, it is true, are opened in Wales, Scotland and Ireland, but the hosts will say that the majority of visitors are from England. Gardening magazines sell in their millions, and millions listen to gardening broadcasts. The English have, we may be sure, inherited an instinct to be growers, even if it is sometimes by proxy.

None of these settlers had braved the crossing of the North Sea to be serfs. Peasants (of a kind) they became, and peasants are not serfs. By owning the soil they tilled and the dwellings they built, they gave birth to the culture of individualism. In no other part of Europe has that same spirit been witnessed, except to some extent in post-revolutionary France. History had to wait a thousand years before another generation of Anglo-Saxons followed suit in North America. The same instinct to ensure a sense of independence by the acquisition of land, it seems, still drives millions to buy their homes and gardens, despite a crippling mortgage, an instinct not shared by others on the Continent, nor even among the Celts.

The system of land tenure, however, had a setback with the Norman Conquest. William I conquered literally: he laid claim to the legal ownership of every square inch of England. To this day his heirs are in strict legal terms the owners of all the land; those we call owners are freehold tenants – tenants who hold the land free of any obligation to a superior title-holder. With the Conquest came a pyramid of tenure; and at the bottom many of the Anglo-Saxon freemen were reduced to serfdom. Nevertheless, expediency now conquered; many of the hides had continued much as before; and the Black Death brought freedom to most of the serfs who survived. Thereafter a landlord and tenant system evolved which prevailed throughout most of England, but it was based on contract and not status as on the Continent in Scotland. The contract was between free men: the tenant was free to farm as he thought fit and to be independent in his everyday life, and in return he paid a rent. Minor clauses might be added – the landlord retaining sporting rights, for instance – but none detracted from his status as a subject of the king, no more and no less than his landlord. It is true that by the time of the Reformation a large proportion of the agricultural land – most historians say it was one-third – was in the hands of the monasteries. It has been said (most vigorously by William Cobbet) that they were model landlords, but neither they nor their successors did much to change the essential fabric of the system. In acquiring so much land, sometimes by questionable means, the abbots depleted the ranks of the freeholders more than otherwise would have been the case, but their tenants still behaved as *coerls*, which was the name given to a freeman in possession of his hide and head of his family. There were other forms of tenure, such as copyhold, which remained until swept away by the 1925 legislation, but none made a major impact upon the evolution of society.

There is a romantic notion about England before the Conquest that its people enjoyed a form of democracy. There are several large grains of truth in that, but Aristotle would have more likely recognised the system of government as what he called aristocracy. The chiefs who led the migration no doubt stayed in charge to organise the settlements, but whether their children succeeded them in the role is another matter. Most probably if the talents of the heir failed to match the father's, another chief was chosen. Later on, we know that even the kings of England were not necessarily the eldest sons of their fathers. There were several instances when the wise men of the kingdom decreed that the rule of primogeniture should be set aside. Between 899 and 1016 AD, eight kings came to the throne; of them only three, Edmund, Eadred and

Eadwig, came by immediate inheritance and agreement, the remaining five being chosen by the wise men.

We know that quite early on social ranks were given different legal privileges. In Kent the *ceorl* was answerable only to the king. He was entitled to compensation from anyone who entered his house unlawfully or seduced his maid servant; and if he himself was killed, the guilty person was required to pay 100 golden shillings (or 2,000 silver pieces) to his family, besides 50 to the king. Among West Saxons the *ceorl* was rather less regarded: his killing required compensation of just half of what it would be in Kent. The rank of *earlcund* was established in Kent also at quite an early stage. Although the *ceorl* was independent of him, an *earlcund* was looked up to as a nobleman, the forerunner of later earls and the counterpart of the Continent's count. To kill such a man was deemed a more serious matter, and the compensation to be paid was three times more than that for a mere *ceorl*. To slay a man on any *earlcund's* estate, the tariff was 12 shillings, but curiously for one of his dependants it was reduced to 6 shillings. To make sure he ranked higher still, the penalty for killing a man on the king's estate rose to 50 shillings. Thus we see the beginning of the three estates of the realm: king, peers and commons. Until the extension of the franchise in the nineteenth century, the commons meant the *ceorls*, or yeomen as they became.[1]

Later on in the Anglo-Saxon age it is evident that the nobility lived and behaved much as the aristocrats in subsequent centuries. Long before the Normans came, they turned away from any kind of work They built themselves great halls where Saturnalia reigned, they kept horses and hounds and hunted the deer, and talked of fighting and war. There is, of course, a rule of human nature: once the money has been piled up by an earlier generation, the sons and grandsons find life so secure that the impulse comes to face risks of another kind.

---

[1] *Geong* is Anglo Saxon for young. A successful *ceorl* had to be as physically fit as a young man.

Any talk of war brought an uneasy relationship between the nobles and the *ceorls*. The latter had work to do on their farms, they had no inclination to abandon their families and leave the responsibility of managing affairs to servants. There were, though, battles to be fought within their island home, for Saxons, Angles, Jutes and Danes were yet to be fused into one nation, and Saxons and Danes had to fight for supremacy. Until all parts of England came under one king, different laws existed and the requirement to leave one's home and serve elsewhere varied from one kingdom to another. The *ceorl* might go not unwillingly to fight for his own king within the frontiers of his territory, for the king's defeat could endanger his own homestead, but a summons to fight beyond would evoke more than just a protest.

Apart from the need to man the *fyrd* (the militia) bridges had to built and fortifications constructed. For these, too, there might be a summons, but the main task force of the *fyrd* would be made up not of *ceorls*; but of their servants and other men who occupied the towns then being established. The *ceorl* can never have been keen to see his servants called from the farm; and that, together with his own reluctance to leave, must have made the king think twice before deciding to fight a war. The attitude of the *ceorls* had a significant effect which endured for centuries. Neither then nor for a thousand years could the kings of England maintain a standing army. "Fight we will but not till our country is in peril," we can hear the *ceorls* declare; and even today, the sentiment echoes still. Unlike the peoples throughout the Continent, the English recoil now as they have always done against military conscription, save only when the enemy is upon them.

The *ceorl* still exists. Somehow with the passage of time he became the yeoman. The Yeoman of England, celebrated in Gilbert and Sullivan's operetta, catches the essence of the man. In the modern economy he is self-employed, vaguely but not entirely middle class, the owner-occupier of unencumbered property. He is independent in spirit, if not in other ways. He is secure enough to be sanguinary-minded. Once personified by

John Bull, he is now less dogmatic; his suit may even be grey, and at his heels is any sort of dog. Today women are *ceorls* too, and there are many who stiffen their husband's backbone, as no doubt they have always done. Beyond the English-speaking world, it is difficult to find many examples of this breed of the human species going back more than a century or two. Holland and the countries of Scandinavia may qualify, but nowhere else and even those robustly democratic nations cannot claim quite so long a tradition as England. In none of the Roman Catholic countries has the spirit of the *ceorl* blossomed out, any more than it has in any of the non-Christian countries. Being a Protestant and believing he can interpret the Bible as he likes comes naturally to a *ceorl*.

When Queen Elizabeth I declared, "I know the people of England, they will ever mistrust their government," she acknowledged that even then the English were not afraid to knock their superiors – if indeed they could recognise anyone as superior. Ownership of his hide, that little bit of England that was his, enabled him to be an individualist. Individualism is more than the antithesis of authoritarianism; it goads one on to mock a government, to revel in satirising it and to cheer the village Hampden. Individualists are dangerous when they speak of others "getting too big for their boots", and when anyone set upon a pedestal hears those words, he should prepare for a fall.

There is one more side to the Anglo-Saxon not to be over-looked. Although the *ceorls* had their land they also had neighbours with similar acreages. As few had substantially more than another, any sense of unfairness or injustice had little cause to arise. Men of equal worth can be on good terms with one another, and be willing, therefore, to cooperate when the need arises. It is an undoubted feature of Anglo-Saxon life that there was a great degree of mutual help. Perhaps this followed naturally from the experiences they shared in crossing the North Sea to a strange land where as pioneers they had to pull together. The same spirit still exists among the prairie farmers of North America where immigrants also shared out the land equally.

Cooperation is next-door to compromising. Again, when we are in a position of equality, in rank if not in wealth, it is easier for us to engage in give-and-take. It has long been shown that a willingness to compromise is an Anglo-Saxon trait. Its existence made possible a remarkable gathering that took place to resolve some differences of opinion over religion, at which a famous compromise was reached whereby religious liberty was tacitly sanctioned and individualism allowed to permeate matters spiritual. The Church of England, it may be said, did not begin with Henry VIII's divorce. The scene was set long ago for the future of England's religion. In 663 AD a great number of clerics gathered at the Abbey of Whitby in Yorkshire, coming from Scotland, Ireland and Wales as well as England, for the avowed purpose of agreeing a date for Easter. In the event the Synod of Whitby evinced a long list of differences in belief and practice within the Church in the British Isles. Although all parts were nominally servient to Rome, the papal writ had gone largely unknown throughout England and totally in the rest of the British Isles for over two centuries. In that time the Celtic countries had gone their own way, departing from the orthodox path in several important instances. They had not built cathedrals as a focal point of clerical power, neither had they appointed bishops nor any hierarchy to be imposed upon the laity. Instead of dioceses and deaneries, monasteries were the centre points and from them went out the monks to perform their priestly and pastoral duties. Their teaching, like their *modus operandi*, was simple and down-to-earth. In the two centuries of freedom, the Celts had moved far away from Rome, and a gulf now divided them from most of England.

Over this Synod presided the King of England. No objective record of the debates has survived and we depend upon loyalists to Rome for what is known. As the debates went on for several weeks we can be sure that much more was discussed than Easter's date. The King, we know, was anxious that his realm was not severed from Rome, and therefore from the Continent. Quite why he wished to be entangled with European affairs we can only speculate. But we do know that among the delegates was a Yorkshire priest called Wilfred, who had travelled widely abroad, and he argued fiercely on behalf of Rome. His main point was that if Britain went her own way she would be cut off from European civilisation and would sink in stagnant isolation. In this there was a grain of truth for the Church was then the mainspring of all learning and scholarship and was to remain so for several centuries.

The outcome was a compromise. Easter's date was harmonised with the rest of Europe, but the other different issues raised were left unresolved. The Celts remained not quite in, yet not quite out of the Roman church. Their aberrations were to be tolerated, and the toleration had its influence upon the English, for such free-thinking within the same island permeated southward, raising doubts here and there; and some have said they prepared the ground for the Reformation. After Whitby, England's church was always just a little semi-detached from Europe's Catholicism.

The year 663 thus saw a formal recognition of religious liberty of a kind not to be known on the Continent for many centuries. In England this liberty had its setbacks, yet even the cruellest of them led to another compromise. When the *Book of Common Prayer* was published it was a compromise of veritable genius, and it is still in use today in scores of parish churches that steer a course between the High and the happy-clappy. And both sides left Whitby unsure whether they were "in Europe".

These pages treat like a concertina five centuries of a country's history; and the generalisations have no pretensions to be anything more than that. However, their purpose is to affirm a truth about why those peasants left their homeland to settle in another country which they could call their own. They were driven by a resolve to be free to till the soil they could call their own, and do it their way and in peace. That is individualism, the conviction that men and women, should be free to do or not do what they wish, unless by common consent it is decided they should behave differently. That is the soil out of which the rest of England's culture has grown.

Their belief in individualism no doubt made those early settlers tough-minded and resolute, and the Saxons especially had a tenacious streak, handling their axe as adroitly as the plough, for it served to slay both humans and animals as well as fell the trees. But they also had a tender side, for in the winter months they would gather around the fire and listen to long epic poems, each learnt by heart by another generation.

A ruthless side of their belief justified them in taking possession of another's land, provided of course it was not already occupied by someone of their own civil society. If that sounds monstrous, it is the same belief that expelled from their homeland countless thousands of native Americans; and many thousands in Australia too, as the Aborigines can testify. This refutes the claim that the two countries have ever been successful examples of a multicultural society. Instead there has been separate development (with the natives left to make the best of the less favourable regions) for which the Afrikaaners had another word. It is a dark side to a culture, explicable if not excusable, and one we must return to in a later chapter.

What is more important for the English is to recognise that the germ of the new culture they brought with them across the North Sea did not belong to the Continent, nor does it belong to it today. In a society divided effectively into lords and serfs, both are given a status; and the status of the serf denies him at birth civic freedom. What civic freedom he subsequently may acquire will be given by way of a grant. The continental lords, though, were collectively the state, with the exclusive power to confer rights upon others. Thus began the need to speak of "human rights", which grant to the governed people freedoms they would otherwise not enjoy. The lords of the feudal system may have vanished long ago, but the European states continue with the notion that rights are something granted. This is quite contrary to how the Angles and the Saxons saw it, for they had quit the Continent to be free men from birth to death with each of them as good as the next man. Chiefs came with them, but the men who succeeded them had to earn their place meritocratically. Of course, at a later stage, as noted already, an aristocracy evolved, but the cardinal belief in individualism survived; it overcame the Conquest and saw off every despot on the throne thereafter.

To offer "human rights", suggesting that they be granted to a people who enjoy the freedom to behave as they wish, subject only to the laws which they have made for themselves – a freedom which their forebears fought and died to protect, often against Continental forces which if victorious would have replaced that freedom with granted rights – is, when one thinks about it, perhaps rather an insult to the English.

Chapter 3

An Island off Europe

Politics, it may be said, is the business of allocating responsibility between the state and the individual. In deciding how to weigh the responsibilities of one against the other there is never likely to be a precise balance. The scales will come down on the side of the state or the individual and the core values and beliefs of a nation will decide which it is to be. So it is with England's culture.

If we pick out the countries that have for more than sixty years – historically a very short time – placed the emphasis on the individual rather than the state, we will find only a few such countries. Is it a coincidence that apart from our Scandinavian kindred (and the Swiss, who are an exception to every rule) they are all in the English-speaking world? All other countries have been subject to some form of authoritarian rule in the twentieth century. All other parts of the Continent, the west as much as the east, have through the ages shared that concept of the state in relation to the individual. So have the Celtic countries, where an historically different attitude was taken towards land ownership, and one similar to much of Europe, especially in the Slavonic east. Scotland, Wales, Ireland and Cornwall knew nothing about primogeniture or the partible distribution of real property. The general principle among the Celts was that land was commonly-held by a family which extended to as many as nine degrees. This meant that rights of ownership belonged to a tribe or clan rather than a family in the English sense. Their integration was such that if one member committed a crime, liability also fell upon a host of cousins to compensate the victim. This communistic philosophy was a far cry from the highly individualistic beliefs of the Angles and Saxons, indeed its antithesis. In an agrarian economy how and by whom land is owned is a determining factor in the nature of a civil society, so that a concept of land tenure will determine the balance between the individual and the state.

When the Pilgrims migrated to what they called New England, the motive was really the same as their Anglo-Saxon forbears. It was in England that the spirit of individualism was born, and a millennium later its near demise led to its rebirth in another England. Tracing this cause-and-effect back to the foundation of England, we find this significant fact of individual land tenure.

Come the Conquest, did not the Normans wipe out this individualism, Europeanising, as it were, the English? There is no simple "yes" or "no". Feudalism of a shadowy kind had developed in England long before 1066. It is, after all, a compact between a peasant and his protector. Even the *ceorl* could scarcely be expected to labour, month after month throughout the year, unless he had some sense of security and reasonable hope that his labours would be rewarded by a harvest safely gathered in. Pre-Conquest England, although a haven of peace compared with the Continent, nevertheless had times when the peasant farmer had need of protection. A warrior-class, with little inclination to sweat in the fields, had emerged from the village elders; they made themselves ready to fight on behalf of their neighbours, receiving a tribute in return. Compacts of this kind had long existed in Europe, and continued to do so long after feudalism ended in England, but on the Continent they were more formalised and tilted in favour of the lord. The Conquest tried to entrench the system, yet it dissolved in the fifteenth and sixteenth centuries, several centuries before it did on the Continent. Why did it dissolve so much earlier than in Scotland, Ireland or on the Continent? In the place of feudalism

40

came capitalism; and the fact that England was the first country to make the change, so long before others, must point to something very significant about either England or the English. The change, after all, brought a transformation that permeated every single aspect of national life. It was not just the whole economy that went through a metamorphosis: another social structure arose and a pristine body of law was conceived to regulate human relationships. So let us see how it was that fate decreed that England should blaze the trail for all others to follow, one by one, over more than a thousand years. That it should happen in a not very large island with a population of some two million ought not to escape a study of the English.

England's history fascinated Karl Marx. Having found the freedom to belabour capitalism in capitalism's mother country, he was intrigued by how it began in the land of his adoption. He noted that England's feudalism was distinctive, particularly in that so many peasants owed no allegiance to a lord. About one-third were freemen, being owners of the land they farmed with the right to dispose of it as they willed. By the sale of land, farms could be amalgamated and the men and women engaged on them made redundant. Driven from the land, they were a workforce to be employed by an enterprising entrepreneur or they were at liberty to set up an enterprise of their own. The right to own private property free of feudal duties afforded the only legal framework in which a capitalist society can function. The peasant miller and peasant weaver, for example, had the protection of the law to quit labouring on the land they held and devote their time to their milling or their weaving. The Englishman could thus be an individualist, a status denied to his Continental counterpart.

In Marx's view, it was this factor that facilitated the transformation from a feudal to a capitalist society more than any other. The Whig historians who did so much to influence the teaching of history, tended to share that view. Neither they nor Marx, had heard the words of Robert Penn Warren: "history is all explained by geography". And the overwhelmingly important fact of

England's geography is her being on an island. Marx in particular failed to delve into why feudalism had been so feebly entrenched in England compared with how it was on the Continent. No frontier was safe over there; the very fact that scores of states and principalities were contiguous led inevitably to one border dispute after another. In the first half of the second millennium, the Continent knew not a single year of peace, for always there was some war between those states, bringing, as all warfare must, insecurity and fear to any farmer within its range. The peasants of Europe had to be protected, so they paid their tributes to their lords and masters to defend them. In that same period, from 1066 to almost the mid-millennium, there was comparative peace throughout the English island. Until the Wars of the Roses, if battles were fought, they were on foreign territory, and it was the land of foreign peasants that was laid waste. The whole *raison d'être* of feudalism so far as the English peasants were concerned ended paradoxically with the Conquest. Of course, the feudal system continued to a degree, but although there were periods of unrest, as in Stephen's reign, the basis of the compact was undermined by a stronger system of central government. The bonds were loosened. The feudal lord, let us remember, lived among his peasants in communities isolated from time immemorial, and gained nothing if he lost their loyalty. Besides, for his income he needed the peasants to cooperate. Feudalism, much maligned by a succession of Whig historians, with Macauley in the lead, as well as by the Marxists, afforded both lord and peasant a system serving a purpose for them both, although no doubt not always as just as it should have been. The English Channel, by giving the islanders protection from the incessant conflicts of the Continent, took away the ground upon which feudalism had been rooted. In so doing, it went a long way towards creating a mercantile system in England before the rest of Europe, with the Industrial Revolution as its sequel, and thence to the immense power of the British Empire. If the reader doubts that history is explained by geography, let us imagine that England's territory was contiguous with that of

France. For a certainty, England would have been as much entangled with the conflicts of the Continent as Flanders. The life for the peasants of England would have been as brutal as it was for the Flemish or the Picardians, and equally in need of a feudal system with its warrior class.

There is a further reason why a mercantile and then a capitalist society began in England. R. H. Tawney in his *Religion and the Rise of Capitalism*[1] and Max Weber in *The Protestant Ethic and the Spirit of Capitalism*[2] have shown how the Reformation brought a change of thinking that went far beyond a narrow view about the Pope. Catholicism is hierarchical, Protestantism individualistic. The former lends itself readily to a feudal structure with levels of authority from a monarch at the summit down to a serf at the base; and to match the temporal regime there is a spiritual empire where Christ's vicar reigns and in which all belief and practice is prescribed. In setting people free to believe and worship differently, the Reformation not only blew away the instinct to obey a superior, but by promoting individualism it engendered self-reliance, and thus an acquisitive mindset. Protestantism made people capitalists by nature. Catholicism, however, fitted a peasant society, for the latter required co-operation among neighbours and it functioned more effectively with a network of extended families. Protestantism is also theologically individualistic. No hierarchy stands between the believer and his God, and the priest-intermediary does not intrude since the Protestant confesses to God directly. He protests the truth of the Bible; with his own eyes he can read the scriptures without a priest-interpreter to tell him what it means. With two or three gathered together, as may be the case today in rural chapels, the Protestants can have their Bible-reading studies, sing their hymns and say their prayers. For the Catholic to feel the full impact of his faith, the processions, sacraments, the swinging of the incense and what might unkindly be called the visual aids all need rather more of a multitude.

[1] R.H. Tawney, *Religion and the Rise of Capitalism*; Transaction Publishers, 1998.

[2] Max Weber, *The Protestant Ethic and the Spirit of Capitalism*; Routledge, 1992.
There are many early editions of both Books.

Protestantism, without a scintilla of doubt, has been a major factor in the making of Englishness. Whether as some have suggested it was the sole determinant, that made England the mother country of modern industrialism is another matter. The latter's seeds were sown long before the Reformation: the wool trade alone proved that. Protestantism, though, suited the Anglo-Saxon temperament. Those early settlers may have come with chiefs and may have worked together in a spirit of co-operation to clear the forests and establish their settlements, but they came to farm their own land, and gain the sense of independence that owner-occupation conveys to us all. On their acres they could be their own men; while the lands their forbears had left behind were still the place that Tactitus had described as no place for peace and quiet.

But would Protestantism have survived if England had been annexed to Europe? Even before the Conquest, successive Popes had tried to cajole the English bishops to toe the line with less ambivalence. Then came Pope Gregory VII and a new vision of Christendom. The world was God's creation. When he sent down his Son it became Christ's kingdom; and as he, the Pope, was Christ's deputy it was his duty to Christ to assume sovereignty over the world. Hence his authority to delegate the administration of temporal matters to the states of Europe, while he retained absolute control over all things spiritual. Powers delegated were powers revocable; what the Pope gave to a king could be taken back. As this sovereignty was passed down to successive Popes, it legitimised action against a monarch who chose to challenge the doctrine of papal sovereignty. What is more, any other king professing loyalty to the church was obliged to assist the Pope in any action against an erring country. From this doctrine has flowed trouble for England that has ebbed around her shores, even to the twenty first century.

Should the English, aided and abetted by the Welsh and Scots, have crossed the Irish Channel to set up what were euphemistically called "plantations"? The twentieth century brought the English many regrets about Ireland, but historians have shown that the Reformation might have failed and England been restored to Rome unless the ascendancy had been imposed upon what Victorians called "John Bull's other island". After Drake had trounced one of the greatest fleets ever to be assembled, Queen Elizabeth must have asked herself what other strategy could Philip of Spain use, at the behest of the Pope, to bring England back into his fold. To build another armada large enough to carry supplies for the soldiers as well as the soldiers themselves would risk another humiliation, yet any invading army would need a supply line. There would be little prospect of a population hostile to Catholicism such as the Welsh being willing to surrender supplies. To Queen Elizabeth it would have been obvious that Ireland was a natural staging-post. In a state of near anarchy after centuries of incessant inter-tribal violence and Catholic to a man, the country could serve Philip's purpose well. In the future perhaps some other army bearing allegiance to the Pope (French, most likely) would receive his orders to invade the island of English infidels, and what a threat an invaded Ireland would be. Even centuries later, the Kaiser, in league with Roger Casement, saw the advantage. Hitler, however, hesitated. De Valera, Ireland's prime minister and a notorious anglophobe, preferred Hitler to Churchill, and it was with his connivance that lights blazed along the Irish coast to guide the Luftwaffe on to Belfast to rain its bombs upon the shipyards; and in the hour of Germany's defeat, De Valera went down to the German Embassy to sign the book of condolences opened on the Fuehrer's death. Whatever the rights or wrongs of the plantations, England after the Reformation was under threat of invasion in the name of Christendom; and another island so near and so given to anarchy as Ireland once was, and in sympathy with the enemy, was plainly a danger. We can imagine that the entire priesthood, and there have always been many priests in Ireland, would have been obliged to summon the people to the aid of the Pope. The doctrines of Pope Gregory VII may have been promulgated some eight centuries ago, but the part they play in England's history rumbles on still.

Let us suppose that Henry VIII had reigned over a segment of the Continent instead of an island fortress. No army would have needed an armada; instead it could have advanced across friendly soil and a simple strategy could have gained the day. Would it also have been necessary for the Pope to cajole Philip into marrying Mary? Before their marriage, many of the English were sceptical about Protestantism and, especially in the north, Catholicism still swayed a large proportion of the people. The twelve years between the death of Henry VIII and the accession of Queen Mary were unhappy times for the English: a little boy king under the thumb of a despot was no prescription to please the people. They knew Mary would be a Catholic queen, yet they applauded wholeheartedly her coronation. She was believed to be strong yet humane, the two qualities that were then most needed on the throne, and indeed initially she was both. But her mother had bequeathed to her a fervent zeal for the true faith. Only too anxious to please the Pope, she married a Spaniard who had the notion that the English could be ruled like his fellow-countrymen. They would succumb to torturing and burning at the stake, he thought, and his wife, believing it would be good for their souls if not for their bodies, concurred. Across the land some four hundred men and women then perished in the flames, witnessed by many thousands. The sublime courage of the martyrs as they renewed their Protestant faith in their dying words had an impact upon the crowds such that neither Mary nor Philip could have comprehended. Nor could they have believed the rippling effect for generations. Queen Elizabeth had many challenges; few were easier to overcome than the Catholic backlash. The martyrs had seen to that. Today nobody ever reads John Foxe's *Acts and Monuments*, commonly called the *Book of Martyrs*.[1] It tells fully with gory, bestial detail of how the martyrs were put to death, but it tells also of their faith. Apart from the Bible it became the most widely read book in the homes of England for over a century;

[1] John Foxe, *Acts and Monuments of Matters Special to the Church*; 3 volumes, The Stationers' Company, 1684.

and in many a house only those two were to be found, placed side by side. Because the accounts that Foxe gives so stirred the emotions while also inspiring the reader to be as brave as his kindred, the *Acts and Monuments* had an influence upon the people of England as much as any other book written, the Bible only excepted. Read by almost every literate person in the land, it whipped up a terrible hatred of what had been done and a fear it could happen again; and for those who could not read, the many pictures of how the torturers did their work ensured that their the passions were no less fierce. Indeed it was the pictures that had the greater impact, so they said, and many a parent took a child by the hand and pointed to what the papists did.

Queen Elizabeth I set England on a course that has been followed until recent times – until, some would say, the beginning of the reign of Queen Elizabeth II. In crossing the oceans to every crevice of the globe, to trade, conquer and rule, the English had to have a springboard, a secure base that would be largely unprotected while her sons went about their business thousands of miles away. Such a base, if sited among jealous neighbours, had to be an island. A single fact of geography goes a long way towards explaining the growth of the Empire, although as it grew, as a later chapter shows, it ceased to be the empire of England.

Although the English can claim no more than half of the island for themselves, the most important part geopolitically is theirs, largely because it is the closest to the Continent. Between one Queen Elizabeth and another, England tended to keep her distance from the rest of Europe and whenever in that long era she found herself entangled in Continental affairs, it seems she usually emerged the poorer.

A disciplined individualism implies a sense of order and a willingness to conform to a few rules so as to bring cohesion to a society without sacrificing the principle of liberty. Preserving this balance has been England's distinctive contribution. Although there have been times when the cause of individual liberty has suffered, it has been when religious zeal has triumphed, as with

Cromwell, or when civil strife has been rampant, as in King Stephen's reign, or threatened as it was by the Jacobins. At other times the English have had few laws to obey and the very limit to their number has given them reason to respect the law. Not for the English the Continental obedience to the spirit of the ordinance, but a firm adherence to its literal interpretation – what lawyers used to call the golden rule. Entry into the European Community and the subsequent cascade of thousands of new regulations has gone a long way to alter an ingrained respect for the law. This is having a radical effect on how individualism and self-discipline are balanced; and hence it is an attack upon the core of Englishness. So long as the European Community edges towards becoming a unitary state, or even a federal union, this central feature of the national character will be at risk.

Chapter 4

A Sense of Justice

We turned to international law to tell us who are the English; and the same branch of jurisprudence reveals a flattering feature of England. Whatever some people may think of how international businessmen behave on the world stage, they are attracted to England as their favoured country for settling legal disputes. The language plays a part in this (perhaps the pleasures of the capital and even the tolerant atmosphere do too) but these international concerns like to have sufficient of their operations in England for the contracts they enter into to be interpreted and enforced according to English law. The London Commercial Court is highly regarded, as are courts that try civil actions generally, as well as the system of arbitration, which is made available as a comparatively cheap and speedy procedure for settling disputes. It is not the even-handedness of the judges or their acute perception or business acumen, such as it may be, that is found admirable, but rather the principles of law that they apply, which is English law (not British, as there is no such thing as British law).

As Pollock and Maitland, in their many-volumed *History of English Law*[1] tells us, the common law began in the year 449 AD when the Jutes landed on the island of Thanet. Both common law and equity, which followed a thousand years later, spring from the same root – the fact that the individual freedom the

[1] Pollock and Maitland, *History of English Law*; Cambridge University Presss, 1895.

first English settlers came to enjoy would be lost unless an Englishman could obtain redress against another when he had suffered an injustice at his hands. The rights that followed under common law are not "top-down", as in a Continental country where the law may have evolved out of a feudal system, but "bottom-up", that is to say not the grant of right by the state but the redress of an individual's grievance at his request on the ground he owed no allegiance to society unless it protected him from injustice. Again we see the influence of the system of land tenure, albeit indirectly, and the consequence of primogeniture. As a result of the latter the individual has no family, tribe or clan to ensure justice on his behalf; instead, by owning his own land he is on an island of his own; and when he is not the eldest son, he must go out into the world to find another island. This dispersal enhanced, rightly or wrongly, individualism, but it also made for vulnerability unless society had laws to protect one individual against another.

The common law has therefore been about contracts and torts. Some have spoken of it as judge-made; but rather it is one precedent built upon another. As regards contracts, it starts from the basic belief that it is in the interests of all honest people that a contract once fairly entered into ought to be enforced. Equally, if someone suffers a tort he should be compensated by whoever committed it. Upon that commonsensical ground has been built over fifteen centuries an edifice of case law in a thousand or more volumes which are also to be found in the United States, Canada, Australia and New Zealand, where judgements can have a persuasive effect upon English courts, and vice versa.

Equity began when someone (or some institution) was first entrusted with property, becoming its legal owner but being required to exercise his rights on behalf of somebody else as the beneficiary. As the years went by trusts and kindred instruments became ever more complicated, and so the difficulty of deciding what is equitable between the trustee and the beneficiary has grown into a considerable body of law unknown on the Continent.

Both the common law and equity have given the courts the duty to protect the individual, but he is also protected against the state by the most grossly misunderstood term used in connection with the law. This concept is that of the rule of law, and it is peculiar to the Anglo-Saxon tradition. Translated into any other language, its meaning is lost, becoming no more than obedience to the law, whatever the law may be. Sadly, this meaning is creeping into the English lexicon; and so a priceless part of the nation's culture is being lost. The essence of the rule of law is that the lawmaker, whether an absolute monarch or an elected parliament, is bound by the law that not even a tyrant can revoke, for it is decreed by God.

The origin goes back to Alfred the Great. In codifying the law of England his first forty-eight clauses were taken from the Bible, so that the Decalogue and the Book of the Covenant were transplanted in a somewhat simplified form into the statute book. Between then and the Conquest there were a number of subsequent codes, which were little more than revised editions or slight amendments to Alfred's legacy. To find any words on today's Statute Book which contradict the original code would be a difficult task.

By the end of Victoria's reign a great body of common law had been built up, precedent upon precedent, pushing out its principles to meet the changes in the lives of the English people. In the twentieth century Parliament superseded parts of the common law with statutes, but as a general rule the principles remain unchanged and the legislation has tended only to remove what had become, over the centuries, anomalous or unforcable. Two notable exceptions stand out: The Leasehold Reform Act of 1993 and the Criminal Justice and Public Order Act 1994. The first gave leaseholders a right to acquire the freehold, regardless of whether the owner was willing to sell. The second changed radically the burden of proof in criminal cases of a sexual nature.

Why are these contrary to the rule of law? The short answer is that both conflict with Christian teaching; but a longer answer is necessary. The rule of law cannot be understood without appreciating how much we are indebted to the church for being the rock on which it is founded. The Conquest of 1066 may have made England not just conquered but legally owned by future kings with absolute power, but their consciences were tempered by a host of clerics who stood beside the king in each of the three areas of governance – legislature, executive and judiciary.

The relationship between the throne and church was never easy; bishops were often the only restraining arm stretching around the monarch, and if stretched too tightly, a head would roll. These clerics had their frailties and not always did they walk in the ways of St Francis, but their office gave them the authority to say the king's will was not God's. There were times when even Henry VIII was thus persuaded to change his mind. Indeed it was in a Year Book in his reign that we can read: "Any law is, or of right ought to be, according to the law of God." And for the law of God they turned to the Bible.

In fact successive English monarchs in the Middle Ages introduced extremely few new laws. What they had inherited was enough for the purpose of good government; and the king's ecclesiastical advisers may well have told him that if his people had required more guidance about how to behave, the good Lord would have let it be known long ago. Besides, there were the manorial courts which had the authority to regulate parochial affairs; and at that time, when most communities lived in isolation, not many matters were of wider concern.

The father of English jurisprudence has been acknowledged as Henry Bracton who lived in the thirteenth century. He laid down the dictum *lex facit regum*, the law makes the king. Bracton held that as the sovereign, the king was supreme and subject to no man, yet subject to God and therefore to God's law. God's law must therefore prevail over the king's.

When James VI of Scotland came to the English throne, bringing from his native country an alien notion of how to rule - the Divine Right of Kings – the jurists had work to do. The greatest among them, Sir Edward Coke, chief justice, who is still quoted in our courts, echoed Bracton's dictum, telling King James that he was under no man, but "under God and the law". For the Stuarts the rule of law had to be spelt out more explicitly. No new decree should be arbitrary, they were told; the law should be clear and the words of a statute have their ordinary meaning, so making ignorance of the law no excuse; no new law should act retrospectively; and all should be equal before the law. "All" included the monarch himself, and since all actions of the government are in his name, it followed that all its branches had to act within the compass of the existing law to the same degree as any individual, and this meant that no part of the government should act arbitrarily. All this flowed effortlessly from God's law.

To be constrained in this way was irksome to the Stuarts. Like their Continental counterparts they saw their role differently: the king made the law and not the law made the king. Since a Protestant is someone who protests the truth of the Bible, it is easier for a Protestant king to accept that the laws should come from the Bible, rather than from the inspiration of a Divine Right. Hence the Glorious Revolution and the Act of Settlement with the stipulation that a Protestant must be king of England and England is to have a constitutional government, as it evolved under the Hanoverians. That the constitution requires the kings and queens to be Protestant may now seem out of date, as well as an affront to Catholics, but the reason goes back to the dispute about what is the mainspring of our laws, whether they stem from the Bible or from something analogous to papal authority.

The advent of constitutional government did nothing to remove the constraint of the rule of law, for the change was intended to do no more than move power from a monarch to a parliament. Now that some of these powers have been passed on to the institutions of the European Union, it might be said that the rule of law has been sharply curtailed, for it has never been a principle of jurisprudence on the Continent where every country, the Scandavia excepted, has endured for centuries life in conflict with England's understanding of the rule of law. This threat to the cultural heritage of England can only be borne by asserting that Parliament has given away no more than a grant to the EU which is revocable in the future.

The Continental view has already made inroads upon our statute law. It may be putting it too emotionally to describe the Leasehold Reform Act as legalised theft, but there are clear grounds on which it offended against the rule of law. In purchasing a lease of property for a period of years from a willing seller, one is undertaking at the end of the term to restore the property to its owner. The Act allows the purchaser in effect to break that contract and deprive the seller of what was lawfully his.

The Criminal Justice and Public Order Act has also overturned a fundamental principle that has hitherto governed our sense of justice. This principle was enshrined by Alfred the Great when he codified the law, and for 1500 years an allegation of a sexual crime has required corroboration before the accused could be convicted. Over the years the corroborative evidence has taken numerous forms. It is not necessarily that of an eye witness, indeed it seldom is, but it must provide confirmation of some material fact relating to the offence. For centuries judges in summing up the evidence have warned juries of the danger of convicting someone of a sexual offence merely on the word of the complainant. They have given powerful reasons why, for example, a woman alleging rape may be fantasising or even wilfully lying. It may be difficult to disprove her story, for it may entail the defendant having to establish his innocence rather than the prosecution having to prove his guilt: and in treating the presumption of innocence of any accused person as a priceless jewel in our criminal law, lawyers have argued that it is better that ten guilty men go free than one innocent man be condemned. I myself know of a man now serving seven years in prison whose "victim" has since confessed that her allegations were untrue. But because her admission was made to a person bound by professional confidence it cannot be used, and an innocent man remains in gaol.

Throughout most of the Continent generally the rules are different. Perhaps they are superior; no doubt they secure more convictions. What Parliament has done is to jettison a principle that jurists have held to be near-sacred (and given the origin, it might be called sacred) so that, as a result of the Act of 1994, a single witness is enough to establish the burden of proof in sexual crimes. This radical change has come about by a coalition: Europeanists have wanted England to be assimilated to Continental ways, and secular humanists are not moved by biblical precepts. Together they are a force, and their influence stretches to most corners of English life. The abolition of *habeas corpus* and the right to be tried by twelve of one's fellow men and women are both on their hit list. Their understanding of the rule of law is not the same as what has been embedded in England's culture for fifteen centuries.

English belief in freedom under the law has been of a particular kind. J S Mill summed it up as the freedom to do as we wish provided we do not impinge upon the freedom of others, but "impinging" is to be taken in its widest sense. When a man was walking down a crowded pavement, recklessly swinging his walking stick, he was asked to desist, and when he replied "This is a free country," he invited the retort "Your freedom ends where my nose begins."

This balanced form of individualism has given the English a respect for the rule of law, but whenever the balance between individual liberty and ordered justice is unduly distorted, as it has been on occasions over the centuries, the consequences can be ugly. Most accounts of the English character note that, though this island people give an appearance of being even-tempered, there is a latent disposition to violence too. Injustice can touch a nerve; gross injustice can summon a mob. The gross injustices in the lives of ordinary people brought violence into the streets on scores of occasions in the eighteenth and nineteenth centuries. In the last half of the twentieth century, it might seem a change came over the English: only the miner's strike and the poll tax riots are examples that come readily to mind. The growth of the welfare state has perhaps gone a long way towards eliminating the social injustices of the past, but now the balance could be distorted by its first cousin – the nanny state with an arsenal of arbitrary decrees.

A few years ago Questions were put down in the House to several ministers asking each of them to list the regulations they had introduced by way of secondary legislation – effectively by-passing Parliament – which contained new criminal offences. Each of the ministers replied in the same way, that there were so many that their number could not be counted. Most of those new laws were the result of directives from Brussels, for which our ministers had only a limited responsibility. Even so, their answers revealed a major upset in the balance between liberty and order. A new crime is about liberty. Thousands of new crimes mean that thousands, if not millions, of people, may go to prison for doing something that they hitherto have done lawfully. Of course, the penalty in the first place will be something far less than a term of imprisonment. Nonetheless, a crime will require the offender to attend a magistrate's court and stand where murderers, burglars and rapists have stood and will stand again; and if they tell the court an injustice is being done and on principle refuse to pay the fine, the magistrates will have their hands forced. The offender will be taken off in a Black Maria, to lose his liberty for a while.

There are over a million men and women in England who run some sort of business; every single one of them has been affected by these new regulations. They have had to act differently because of them, and to that extent their freedom has been curtailed. Perhaps some of them agree that the new laws are just, that is to say that they should not have acted in the way they did before the new crimes were introduced. The rest of the businessmen, whose number will be not far short of a million, have submitted to the new bureaucratic will. There is, though, more straw to be piled on the camel's back. Our friends in Whitehall and Brussels who think up these new laws are never likely to complain that they have nothing more to do and admit they have become redundant. So as the years go by, there will be more bits of straw. Who dares believe that these hundreds of thousands of businessmen and women – *ceorls* all – will bear the burden uncomplainingly?

There is an alternative scenario. Indeed, it is unfolding already. If a new regulation seems unnecessary, unjust, unenforceable or ignorable – well, let's just drop it in the bin. This is how they behave, so the English are told, on the Continent, and as Britain is "in Europe" they begin to do the same. Out goes the golden rule about the literal interpretation of the law, and in comes obedience to its spirit; and the objective test gives way to the subjective. This has two dangers. First, it means that the individual has a licence to decide whether the law is really intended to apply to him or to what he would like to do. The second is more perilous to the country's governance. The lay magistrates will begin administering justice also in a subjective way which could lead to an appellate system far beyond what exists today. Then the professional judges will find that they too must conform to the new philosophy. England has always distinguished the role of the judicature from that of the legislature, and for a very sound reason. Only Parliament, the elected representatives of the people, should decide what laws should be obeyed, for they can be made accountable to the electorate for the liberties lost. For anyone else to make our laws is essentially undemocratic. On the Continent this principle has never been digested, and as a later chapter shows, the European interlude is making the English throw up what over the centuries they themselves have digested. This highlights how delicate is the balance between individual freedom and ordered justice; both abstract terms are difficult to define, yet upon achieving the right balance depends a respect for the law. Once that respect is lost, lawlessness is not far behind. Lost too is over a thousand years of Englishness.

Of the distinctive features of England's culture, there is one that surely must be significant in delineating the character of her people. It is not just the number of religions, but all their various branches and denominations, splinters and chips off the block that seemingly prosper. The immigration of Jews and Moslems bears witness to the way that no sooner does a major wave of other religionists come here than the discipline of their orthodoxy tends to weaken. Both of those faiths have notable qualities, but foremost among them is probably not latitudinarianism. To accuse the English climate or the landscape or any of the country's physical features for any breakdown of discipline would be rather fanciful, so it must be something to do with the English people. The intermingling or the daily contact with others of a different culture – the rubbing-off of Englishness – seems the only obvious reason. The chatterati who cannot bring themselves to say a word in favour of the English will insist it is the British influence. This will not do, since the British have not been tolerant about religion. Calvinism in one form or another prevails over most of Scotland, and even in the industrial heartland its ethic is evident, and tolerance is not the most obvious attribute of Calvinism. In the case of the Welsh, an outward show of insouciance conceals an inner commitment to "the truth", never to be underestimated. As for the remaining British across the water, the chatterati who abide the Ulstermen even less than they do the English will be hard-pressed to claim more tolerance in Northern Ireland. No, it is in England and not in the rest of Britain that this splintering prospers. And in the case of Christianity it has done so to an inordinate degree.

For an explanation this schismatic tendency we need look no further than to English individualism. Is there another country, whatever its size, that exceeds England in stretching out a tolerant hand to as many religions and to so many of their sects and denominations? We might imagine the United States, the haven for the persecuted, to be high in the league, but their immigration rules having limited the number of Indians, most of the sub-continent's faiths are still to be represented. The American diversity exists obviously in certain states, New York and California in particular, but in others which are overwhelmingly Protestant the schisms tend to be only in that one branch of Christianity. It is in England rather than the United

States that a more widely spread diversity of religion is found, and it is to her shores all religions have come, excepting only those of the most primitive peoples. Even cults of questionable repute have built their citadels and chapter houses; and planning officials are said to display more indulgence to them than to their own fellow-countrymen.

Why then is this small country host to such diversity? To point out periods in England's history when intolerance was rampant is easy enough. The most notable of them (anti-Catholic fervour) has already been alluded to, and one hopes in its true context. When a people are told that war has been declared upon their country by the head of a church, it is not unnatural for them to assume that its priests are also his spies; and anyone consorting with spies must themselves be suspect.

Suspicion about Roman Catholicism lingered on; that mass for the English had to be in a foreign language did not help, nor the fact that the head of the Church was always an Italian. Now the Vatican has washed away the grounds of suspicion and Anglicans, Methodists and many others will kneel down with Roman Catholics; and for the latter to enter another's church is no longer a sin.

Both Jews and Nonconformists also suffered intolerance. Both were excluded from Parliament and the universities; and long ago all Jews were summarily expelled from England until readmitted by Cromwell. The first of the Jews to return settled in the City and became bankers. Lombard Street is a name to testify to the City's welcome for the immigrant. The merchant banks have always had a central role in the City's fortunes, and none, it is said, was founded by an Anglo-Saxon. This suggests that the Dutch, Germans and French as well as the Jews found toleration in the Square Mile if nowhere else. That both Parliament and the universities were the preserve of the Church of England is a manifest injustice to our eyes today. In the case of the former one may plead the union of church and state as the foundation for the nation's stability, although a cynic would say with some justification that the exclusion was more to do with the retention of power. On the other hand, until the Toleration Act was passed, England was continually under threat, and successive sovereigns had reason to believe that the country's enemies, France in particular, had recruited agents in this country. Jews were suspiciously international and non-conformists suspiciously radical – both fertile grounds for prejudice against them. As to the universities, they practised exclusion on the pretext that they were Church foundations; fortunes had been left them because they provided an Anglican education. This was more or less true.

Yet towards the end of the nineteenth century, waves of Jewish migrants from the east of Europe came to England to seek asylum. They spoke no English but a strange language; they wore strange clothes; they ate strange food; they had strange habits, like working on Sundays but not Saturdays; and initially (and naturally) they kept to themselves. Yet within just a few decades those who wished to be assimilated had been accepted totally. A quarter of Mrs Thatcher's Cabinet were descendants of those immigrants, so were three Lord Chief Justices and a large proportion of the rest of England's judiciary, as well as masters of Oxford and Cambridge colleges and presidents of learned societies, and even a bishop of the established Church. In every citadel they sit at the top table. It is doubtful whether they would have gained comparable heights in Scotland, Wales or Ireland, any more than they would have done in France or Germany.

In France they suffered as much as they did in Germany. When the French changed sides in the war the French government ordered the Jews to be rounded up in their tens of thousands to be sent to Hitler's camps. Among the Frenchmen who volunteered to do Hitler's work was a young man called Mitterand, decorated by Pétain for these services, and his fellow countrymen deemed it no bar to the nation's presidency, while Herr Kohl chose him as his closest ally. As a haven for hundreds of thousands in earlier centuries England was seen as a natural alternative to the United States.

What is more, several times immigrants have gone straight to the uppermost pinnacle of the Establishment. Since 1066 the English have enthroned a succession of foreigners usually with much rejoicing. Three of them came to be rulers with absolute powers over their subjects. To welcome and then submit to an alien from abroad to preside over their destiny must surely be the ultimate symptom of a tolerant people.

Huguenots and Jews have found on these shores religious freedom, and there is no evidence that the same is denied to the hundreds of thousands of Moslems and Hindus who have come in recent years. Now more worship in the mosques of Peterborough and Bradford than the total who do in the churches, chapels and cathedrals of those two cities. The same is probably true in many other towns in England where Moslems have settled in large numbers. An insignificant minority has gone to Wales and Scotland, perhaps not one per cent of the total, which is out of all proportion to the populations of the three countries.

With some two million Moslems, a considerable number of orthodox Jews and members of other religions that are not Christian, together with an uncountable number of non-believers, is it still realistic to speak of England as a Christian country? It is a dangerous word to use; even the local vicar and the Baptist minister will define a Christian differently. The ordinary person, though, unconnected with any church, will use the word to give the highest praise about how someone has behaved. He speaks of a Christian in a moral sense, as living by the rules of life laid down in the Sermon on the Mount; and above all, about how we should treat other people. This allows us to make England a plural society when it comes to religious observance. Thomas Jefferson summed up the principle: "It does me no injury if my neighbour claims there are twenty gods or only one God."

Nonetheless, by invoking Christian ethics as a guide to our conduct and to deciding what laws are made to regulate our behaviour towards others, we step upon thin ice. Not even Christians can agree upon issues such as abortion, divorce, homosexuality, and capital punishment. So in a religiously plural society can common ground be found? If not, upon what ethical principles is it possible to place not just the nation's laws on moral issues, but the code of behaviour generally that a nation can unite upon and accept as the norm?

In the innumerable articles, lectures and politicians' speeches as well as sermons and even full length books on the merit of a multicultural society, the question never seems to have an answer. Yet if harmony is to prevail in a religiously plural society, it is surely time a decision is made. Perhaps an initiative should come from the churches themselves; and this author is diffident about going where those angels fear to tread. The very origins of the English made them latently a Protestant people. Their individualism found a natural home in a creed that removed a priestly intermediary between the individual and his God, and set him free to read God's word as he chose. Protestantism, being, one might say, theological individualism, is inevitably schismatic. Between Henry VIII's theology, which when read by the Pope, earned him the title of Defender of the Faith and Cromwell's muscular beliefs, there was little meeting point. Yet there was and remains a thread that weaves its way through the inconsistencies. For Christians it is in the Bible that God's word must be found and although the two testaments may afford a feast for debate, there is one passage that all are forced to agree upon – the Sermon on the Mount. Neither Henry VIII nor Cromwell would have asserted with much conviction that they lived up to its precepts, but neither would have denied it was God's guidance about how we should live.

It is not such a simple message as it seems when read for the first time, especially the fuller version in St Matthew's Gospel. Nevertheless, with a few recent exceptions alluded to already, the thousands of England's laws and ordinances do not contradict what it tells us. Since the primary legislators in Parliament or the secondary ones in Whitehall are unlikely to have gone through the Sermon each time to draft their new decree according to His word, we can assume their hands have been guided by an ingrained cast of mind born of Christian teaching.

A careful reading of the Sermon shows that Jesus was qualifying and sometimes almost contradicting passages in the Old Testament which may cause an orthodox Jew to raise an eyebrow. Many Moslems may find it difficult to endorse parts of the Sermon. Rationalists too may balk at swallowing some of it. So if we are to be a morally as well as a religiously plural society, this places us in a difficulty. We overcome it only in one of two ways: either the English become a nation of relativists and they choose the moral precepts that they happen to find agreeable, or they apply a plain democratic principle and insist that a majority view prevails. This does not mean that we should take no account of the beliefs of minorities. Islam, for example, can teach us lessons that we would do well to learn. But in the end it is important for any society to arrive at a consensus, and in a democratic society this has to be one that carries conviction to the majority of its citizens. Minorities, and indeed individuals, are quite entitled to dissent, and in minor matters some pushing of the boundaries can be beneficial. If many twentieth-century women had not decided to wear fewer clothes than their mothers thought proper, young women today would still be dressed like their Edwardian great grandmothers. Nevertheless, there are strict limits to this and no one is entitled to act in ways that have been made illegal by the host community – say female circumcision or forced marriage – on the grounds that such practices are normal where they come from.

No doubt some immigrants will protest; their leaders will raise yet again the cry of racialism, and an echo will come from pressure groups peddling any absurd form of political correctness. It is extremely important to meet this challenge. The freedom to worship as we will, the freedom to associate with whom we wish and the freedom to speak our mind all spring from the principle of toleration. The two latter freedoms are qualified, but only on the libertarian ground that one man's freedom must respect that of others. To suit their own book one government after another, even in recent memory, has sought to inhibit public criticism. The kindred freedoms, those of the press, and of the House of Commons, where members have the unique privilege to say what they believe, have between them succeeded in frustrating those knavish tricks of government. As a core value, though, it is no more than superficially safe; and among its enemies are bodies purporting to represent immigrants from countries where freedom of speech is denied, and where government critics go to prison.

Political correctness is *de facto* censorship; in its extreme form it is fascist-minded and its proponents often show little regard for toleration in other areas beyond the use of words. It had its origin in a respect for the feelings of other people or what might be called simple good manners, but the doctrine – for such it is – has become a weapon in the hands of minorities with the political motive of denying a majority the right to express its opinion, and is thus inherently undemocratic. Political extremists, in particular Trotskyists, have infiltrated immigrant bodies to play the race card and have set out wilfully to incite racial consciousness. This has had the pernicious effect of widening the gulf between black and white, with the patently obvious aim, since they are professed revolutionaries, of promoting discord. A later chapter sets this out in some detail. In this way a move towards tolerance of newcomers becomes perverted into a drive towards intolerance of the majority. If it succeeds it will seriously erode our freedoms, freedoms which did not originate in the Magna Carta, nor in any code or constitution, nor in a Bill of Rights which only reaffirmed what was established centuries before. It was the original immigrants to this island, the Angles and the Saxons, who brought with them the assumption that these freedoms belonged to the individual. That's why they came.

Chapter 5
An English Philosophy

Opinion about philosophy, as Isiah Berlin said, varies between those who claim it as the queen of science and others who dismiss it as no more valuable than astrology or alchemy. Nevertheless, it is common ground that philosophy has been the seed-bed where our forbears cultivated political and moral principles; and so a people with a distinctive philosophy must themselves have a distinctive culture. And the English are such a people. Not many nations can claim a similar distinction. The Germans are idealists (in the sense philosophers use the word, one ought to add) in the tradition of Kant, Fichte, Schelling and Nietzsche among others, while in France there are rationalists, like Leibnitz, Voltaire and Rousseau. India, China and Japan also have their distinctive schools of thought. The idealists could only have been German, and the rationalists had to be French. Although these philosophers influenced their fellow countrymen, it has to be said with greater force that the temperaments of the two nations are captured in what their philosophers have written.

The English, though, tend to shy away from philosophy. In the universities it attracts few students; and we do not hear in cafés, even in Bloomsbury, heated debates about metaphysics, as we can in Paris. Abstract terms are not for the English. What can be seen and touched, the real and sensually experienced, is for them what can be usefully talked about and end in sensible decisions. Thus out of the English mind has come a school of thought to which it may claim a proprietary right – empiricism.

It is the mimesis of a nation's temperment, as rationalism is of the French and idealism of the Germans. When the Americans took up philosophy, they imported empiricism, and characteristically brought it down to earth, calling their version at first radical empiricism, and later pragmatism. Borrowing the language of Wall Street with words like "profits", "results" and "cash-value" it has been a mirror of the New World's values. In the hands of such thinkers as William James and John Dewey, pragmatism belongs to Uncle Sam as much as Mom's apple pie.

So what is this empiricism? Aristotle may be given some credit for the genesis, and also the remarkable School of Alexandria. This port in Aristotle's lifetime had become the centre of international trade and in linking Europe with the Orient it became a city where East and West engaged in intellectual as well as commercial intercourse. Its School attracted many thousands of students from far away. Not only did the library amass some 700,000 books, but its zoology department gathered every known species of animal and its botanical gardens kept every discovered plant, and in all the sciences it excelled. But just as Aristotle collected an immense amount of data so did the School; neither marshalled the mass into satisfactory hypotheses or laws as a scientist does today. That great step forward was left for a thousand years. Such was the tragedy of a civilisation destroyed and the subsequent monopoly of learning held by a Church hostile to science.

The awakening came, so historians tell us, with an Englishman, Roger Bacon (1214 – 1292), a scientifically minded monk. But it was Francis Bacon (1561-1626) – no relation to Roger – who really unshackled philosophy from its chains, setting it free to advance over the following centuries. Today he is better known for his *Essays*[1], but his work on philosophy, was of immense importance in setting not just philosophy but science itself on its future course, and for over a century the two

---

[1] Of the many editions the one in the Everyman's Library may be the most readily available.

were treated as one, science being known as natural philosophy. "Nature cannot be commanded," he wrote, "except by being obeyed." This could not be done by deduction or pure reasoning as the Greeks had tried to do, and as the rationalists and idealists of Europe still do, but by induction or inferring a general principle from particular facts. The facts, he said, are gathered from one's own research or experience – hence he can be hailed as the father of empiricism.

To embark on this new journey the mind must first be purged of all prejudice and pre-conditions. Idols he called them. First came the Idols of the Tribe. Imagination can lead us astray, for the image of anything that may be accepted by the society in which we belong may not be its reality. As we grow up and throughout adulthood we tend to assume that the long-held beliefs of others are true; this is not good enough, we should take nothing "as read". Allow one of these ideas into one's reasoning, without it being established to one's own empirical satisfaction, and a series of errors may follow to wreck the whole process of induction.

Then there are the Idols of the Cave. "Everyone," said Bacon, "can have a cave or den of his own," and into this have come his own ideas and images that he has had no need to verify beyond reasonable doubt. Some of us, he adds, are disposed towards antiquity, others to novelty or the "just medium". As we go through life, we all collect a lot of baggage, and no two of us may have exactly the same collection, for the possible combinations are infinite. However fond we may be of our collection, the whole lot must go if we are to find truth.

Thirdly come the Idols of the Market Place. In our everyday life we mix with others with whom we share a common language. Necessary though this may be, there is a danger in using words "according to the understanding of the crowd" as Bacon put it. It is with words one tells lies and, what may be worse, half truths, for they can be more difficult to detect. Words, then, are all-important to the philosopher and they must be chosen carefully, regardless of the crowd.

Last are the Idols of the Theatre. "All the received systems of philosophy," declares Bacon, "are but so many stage plays." Living in a dream world of their own making, philosophers have conjured up unreality as poets and dramatists have done. Theirs has been a world of dogma and deduction, influencing the rest of us in ways of which we may scarcely be conscious. So these Idols are just as dangerous as the others.

Even today it remains a tall order to cleanse our thinking of these Idols, but four centuries ago when all learning had been in the hands of deductive theologians, so that every branch of knowledge was ingrained with their teaching, it was beyond the realm of the possible, even for Bacon himself. But this remark-able man, diplomat, politician, public prosecutor, Lord Chancellor, essayist, scientist and philosopher – but sadly a fraudster too – set philosophy in England along its path, and a different one from the rest of the world.

Thomas Hobbes (1588-1679) visited Bacon on several occa-sions and undoubtedly was influenced by him. Both agreed that method was the key to knowledge, and knowledge led to power, but Hobbes did not dismiss the value of pure reason. In this respect he is not always counted among the empiricists, although when it came to politics, the sphere in which he is principally remembered, his views were unquestionably coloured by his direct experiences. No English philosopher lived in more turbulent times, none had his liberty or even his neck more at risk; and as soon as Parliament voted to impeach Strafford, Hobbes made off to the Continent. Thereafter he claimed that he was the "first of all that fled". Despite being an avowed Royalist and later accused of atheism at a time of reli-gious zeal, he managed to survive. Indeed, he did rather well living to the age of ninety-one, outliving his adversaries and leaving behind a body of erudite works as extensive as any modern philosopher.

His political thought has been seriously misunderstood: he never argued for a monarchy with sovereign power over a nation as the only ideal form of government. What he did say was that there should be sovereignty, and that it should vest in either a monarchy or a parliament. We still debate this issue of sovereignty, its nature and who should exercise its powers. Indeed, the issue is the heart of the argument about our membership of the European Union. Hobbes may have died three centuries ago, yet his legacy endures: it does much to distinguish how the English see the European Union from the view held by the rest of the Continent.

To reach his conclusions about sovereignty quite a long journey has to be undertaken through the labyrinths of geometry, mechanics, psychology and ethics, as well as the elements of politics itself. Why on earth geometry? Not until he was forty did this tutor to the Cavendish family show much interest in philosophy; and at Oxford, where attempts were made to instill the wisdom of Aristotle (presented as the last word in the subject, which in a sense it was) he reacted violently against the Aristotelian method. Then years later he happened to pick up a book on geometry. He marvelled at some of the proofs, for they proved all sorts of propositions that he did not think were provable. Deductive or no, they persuaded him that here were tools to be used. But tools are useless in the void, they must be put to work on something solid and empirical.

Natural philosophy at bottom is about causes and effects; causes move to effects and effects become causes, which move to further effects. The essence of this is motion. The world of nature, then, is about motion, which is the principle that pervades all life, all activity and everything that matters. As no facet of philosophy can escape this principle, we can make it the starting point in working out a system of ethics. Ethics is about our behaviour, but how we behave is decided by what is in our minds. So what makes us do one thing and not another, or why do we avoid or decline acting in a particular way? Again, this according to Hobbes is a matter of motion. Our mind propels us into action, either moving towards some deed or away from it. We move forward because our sensations and their associations assembled in our minds have made it desirable to do so. Desire is an expression of our appetite, so Hobbes concludes it is our appetite for something that leads us to a positive action. Then there is the opposite decision by the mind when we move away or avoid a form of activity, because our sensations have taught us an aversion towards it. Hobbes denied there could be a third kind of motion in our behaviour. Either we did something or we didn't: even if we half-did something we would move forward and then draw back. Thus all our behaviour, whether positive or negative, is governed by our appetites and aversions.

Hobbes paints a dismal view of human nature. We are not exactly flattered by what he thinks about us for we are made egocentric and self-seeking. Love, pity, compassion and any other feelings that enhance human relationships and make for the happiness of others are not denied. They exist all right, but we express them out of self-concern. We love because we want to be loved, and when we show our grief, it only shows our sense of loss. For showing the better side of our nature, we expect to be given something in return. Sir Robert Walpole echoed Hobbes when he looked around the House of Commons and declared "Every man has his price."

As for those ignoble qualities that can well up in all of us, like hatred, greed and untruthfulness, these spring from another collection of appetites and aversions. True, we may try to curb these instincts and even succeed in doing so, but our success is a measure of our fear of the consequences. Just as our appetite leads to pleasure, so our aversions give us pain. Everything we do or not do will lead to at least some degree of pleasure or pain; and nothing of any consequence leaves us with a truly neutral sensation. There may be many occasions when our emotions are complex, with both pleasurable and painful sensations, or a blend together of pleasure and pain, but no matter the complexity of these, we are left with a net effect, a bottom line where there is a degree of more pleasure or more pain in the total sum of sensations.

Such a theory of psychology needs only a short leap towards a system of ethics. As human beings act only out of self-concern, it means that society is in a state of warfare between all its parts. Tough measures are called for, and without them the life of man becomes, in Hobbes' words, "solitary, poor, nasty, brutish and short". Without such measures there can be little hard work done without immediate payment, no plans for future well-being, no more expansion of learning or cultivation of the arts; and no purpose in fine architecture for another generation to admire or in literature for others to appreciate. Any of these may gratify our self-love, but the pain of making the effort may outweigh the appetite. So no pussyfooting; we must submit to tough measures in order to live in peace with one another.

As it is in our interests not to suffer from the appetites and aversions of others, and it is not enough for only a few of us to agree to what is in our self-interest, all of us must either agree or be deemed to agree to the laws governing our behaviour. Yet we cannot expect all our fellow men and women to accept that it is in their self-interest to change the way they behave unless they are confident that others will do the same. Some power must therefore exist to make sure the change is made secure. That entails a power greater than what any individual or group can put together. Powers of coercion to order and compel must thereafter reside in some entity other than just a group of people. To be fully effective coercion must come from a supreme or sovereign power. Hence a social contract between the governed and a government, with the former surrendering their freedom, given by nature, to behave according to their appetites and aversions, in return for protection by the government.

Whether the government resides in a single individual or a representative body of individuals is a question to be decided by the circumstances in which a society finds itself. In a state of unbridled conflict, widespread disorder or a major war, for example, dictatorial powers may be unavoidable. Given a state of tranquillity, a representative form of government can safely be entrusted with the sovereign power. That, one may say, is obvious.

Obvious or not, it is not the case in England today. The United Kingdom, having entered the European Union, has become part of a system where the sovereign powers of coercion that are needed to prevent our lives becoming "solitary, poor, nasty, brutish and short" are no longer resting solely in a parliament representative of the people to be governed. The contract has been broken.

Sovereignty has five elements. There is the sovereign – or supreme – power to make laws as well as to interpret and enforce them. There is also the power to tax or take away our lawfully gained money. Then there comes the power to enter into treaties with other countries and the power to declare war. In each case these powers are sovereign when there is no higher power.

William's conquest of England brought all these powers into his hands exclusively. He and his Norman successors were the sovereign power. The political history of England has been about how power gradually left the monarch to rest with a representative parliament directly answerable to the people over whom they exercise those powers. Of those powers only one has its sovereignty retained within the United Kingdom – the power to declare war.

Although the concept of the social contract had some currency in France, only in Hobbes' version was the notion of sovereignty understood. What the English people lost in the Conquest but regained over centuries of civil conflict has been lost again.

Does it really matter? The Hobbesian argument can be put quite shortly. Man in his natural state was born free to do what he liked in so far as he had the power to do it. That power can be taken away in times of peace and tranquillity and given to others if he can choose them as being capable of protecting him, and they make themselves answerable to him for what they do for his protection. Hobbes would have called that parliamentary government. We may speak of it now as democracy, but in Hobbes' time that word had Aristotle's meaning, the rule of the mob or what today we would call direct democracy. He would have said there can be no valid social contract between the governed and the government when the sovereignty over the governed passes into the hands of unelected people in another country. To Hobbes their powers, therefore, would have had no validity.

Hobbes was followed by John Locke (1632-1704) who is generally said to have been the true founder of empiricism. Professor Rogers, an American, in his *History of Philosophy*[1] wrote of Locke that he stood for all that is most characteristic of English philosophy. His life was not quite so turbulent as Hobbes', although he too had to flee to the Continent for asylum, and did so twice. On another occasion he was dismissed from Oxford despite holding a post for life. Again, like Hobbes, he reacted against Oxford's teaching of philosophy, then still imbued by scholasticism, and did not take up its study until middle age.

To speak of knowledge as something self-evidently useful and a means to any kind of power is not enough, he said. There is little point in knowledge unless we can rely upon it, and to be reliable it must be verifiable, and what we can vouch for. We cannot be born with such knowledge, for at the moment of birth we can vouch for nothing. So, he argued, we have no innate ideas, and even if we did, we cannot count them as knowledge for we cannot verify their truth. Instead we came into the world as if a blank piece of paper. Immediately on arrival we have sensations and as we grow up we develop our different senses that provide the sensations. It is from these and from them alone that we gain our knowledge as our blank piece of paper is gradually filled up with what we are told by our senses and what is verified by them. The philosopher who shuts himself up in his study to write his books with each proposition leading to the next by pure reasoning will reach conclusions that none of us should trust. That is what the Continentals and the Germans in particular do, Locke would have said. Far better, he would add, to go out into the real world and let our senses get to work. That is certainly what Locke did himself.

[1] Arthur Rogers, *History of Philosophy*; Macmillan & Co, New York, 1962.

Although his fame stems mainly from his theory of knowledge set out in his *Essay Concerning Human Knowledge*[1], his political philosophy in many ways ranks more highly. Not only was it derived largely from his own experiences in public life, but it put the case for the Glorious Revolution that gave England a constitutional monarchy, while at the same time it laid out the liberal principles of government with its emphasis on toleration and freedom of both speech and religion; and if those principles are quintessentially English, then its beneficiaries owe a major debt to Locke. It should be added that his political writings, especially the *Second Treatise of Civil Government*[2] were well known to the architects of both the French and American revolutions, and when the Declaration of Independence was drafted, Thomas Jefferson came rather close to plagiarism.

As Hobbes was a pessimist about human nature, so Locke was an optimist. The difference between the two men's principles springs almost entirely from that; yet their views on moral philosophy were not dissimilar. Hobbes held that there could be no absolute standards about good and evil. What Jones considers good may be evil in the mind of Brown, and what Brown believes to be evil may be neither good nor evil for Smith. I think it was Professor Ayer who used to say that each one of the Ten Commandments is challenged in the moral code of a community somewhere in the world.

In Hobbes' view whatever induced our pleasure was good, and evil was whatever gave us pain. Locke shared Hobbes' dichotomy, and goes on to explain how it comes about. We arrive in the world without any knowledge of morals; the sensations record on our blank piece of paper what we find pleasurable or painful. As babies, learning how to seek one and shun the other, we are guided by adults, mothers especially, and later on by our fellow children. What we are told by them is not what we may know personally. We do not have to be stung by a wasp to be sure we ought to keep away from the wasps' nest at the bottom of the

---

[1] John Locke, *Essay Concerning Human Knowledge*; Everyman Library, 1993.

[2] John Locke, *Second Treatise of Civil Government*; Davidsons, 1982.

garden. We soon learn that it is wrong to steal or tell lies and because that seems self-evident to us we are likely to believe we are born with the innate notion that they are acts of wrongdoing. Locke denies that this can be so. The notion that stealing and telling lies are wrong has been held for so long in our society, without it being questioned, that it has become ingrained in our thoughts, and even deemed to be placed in our minds by a divine power.

God plays a part in this; if nature is His manifestation, He has decided what for each of us is good or evil according to our sensations, having made one pleasurable and the other painful. Nature, though, has not been helpful to us in deciding objectively the difference between good and evil, simply because Jones and Brown have different sensations about pleasure and pain; and the more we differ among ourselves, the greater the need for a system of law to decide how we should behave. Locke spoke of three groups of laws. There are divine laws, and we are in breach of them when we commit a sin. Our punishment is a matter for conscience – or the hereafter. They are not the same as crimes or laws introduced by an agency of the state, for these will vary from one state to another and the state will enforce the law and punish the offender. There are also, said Locke, laws of opinion. In every society there are many things that general opinion considers should be done or not done. Here the sanction is a reputation lost.

Locke maintained that man in his natural state had good reason to behave well, for much of what he wanted was his by natural right. He could speak his mind and worship as his conscience led him; he had the liberty to move from one place to another and was able to claim property as his own. Nor was he at war with the rest of the world, as Hobbes had believed.

However, the exercise of these natural rights is subject to other men also claiming them. Travel freely he might, but if he sought shelter in another's cave, his claim might be contested by an indignant occupier stronger than himself. As Hobbes pointed out, freedom whether in nature or otherwise is of little value unless it can be protected by some institution more powerful than those who may dispute it. However, says Locke, since most people behave reasonably well, human nature need not be controlled beyond certain modest limits. "No-one," said Locke, "should harm another in life, health, liberty and his possessions," so the rule of the state is restricted to preventing such harms being done. For generations of libertarians his words have been music to their ears. Curtailing the role of government to preventing harm being done to those rights means upholding the idea of the minimalist state. Such modest powers as a government needs were divided by Locke into three. Laws had to be made, they had to be interpreted and enforced, and they had to be administered. In this division he foreshadowed Montesquieu's separation of powers between the legislature, judiciary and executive, but he did not go so far as to propose that they should be strictly separated.

The English, more than most, have been property-conscious. Only in England (never in Scotland) does one see "Trespassers will be Prosecuted". The concern for property is shown in other ways too, like the high proportion of owner-occupied houses, even though they may be mortgaged for half a lifetime. Into the middle of the twentieth century an Englishman who amassed a million or two was entitled to a peerage on the ground that his stake in the country's fortunes had become so large that he should have a greater opportunity of protecting it. In fact, William Pitt fixed £100,000 as the point when there was a right to a peerage. Locke gave weight to the sentiment when he wrote: "The great and chief end of men uniting into commonwealths and putting themselves under government is the possession of their property."

A man's property is an extension of himself. Whatever he has acquired by his skill and industry should be his to keep or dispose of as he wishes. An inheritance is property received from a benefactor who chose to pass it on in that way, so property inherited should also be kept in the hands of the heir for as long as he desires. Locke saw no justice in the redistribution of wealth.

Like Hobbes he believed in a social contract implicit in the relationship between the governed and the governors. It led him to explore how far the governors would be corrupted by the power vested in them. His conclusion that the powers of government should be diffused between its three arms has resonated ever since among constitutional lawyers. The power to make laws that others must obey on pain of losing their liberty was not to be treated lightly, an opinion that held sway in England for two and a half centuries after his death. No law should be passed, he contended, without most careful consideration, and in every case it must be approved by representatives elected by the people. A law made in any other way was not one that could be respected by those who had to obey it. The abuse of power by the government could best be avoided by making the legislature the supreme authority able to override both the executive and the judiciary. After all, the legislators were chosen by the people and answerable to them; and if the people felt aggrieved they had recourse to those they had elected to protect them. This principle of accountability to those coerced by laws passed and taxes levied has sadly never taken a firm root outside the English-speaking world.

Locke was followed by a long succession of English philosophers whose influence continues to this day. They were all empiricists, although two of them rather wandered off into the realm of German idealism. They were T. H Green (1836-1882) and F. H. Bradley (1846-1924). Neither had much of a following, so it can be said of English philosophers that despite their large number, they have been remarkably consistent.

In the same century as Green and Bradley were Bentham and Mill. Jeremy Bentham (1748-1832) followed the English tradition that our actions were governed by the degrees of pleasure or pain they caused us. As he put it "nature has placed mankind under the governance of two sovereign masters, pain and pleasure...they govern us in all we do, in all we say and in all we think." There is no inherent virtue or merit in any thought or action, but in how it affects our feelings. If our action touches no one's feelings but our own, it is then a matter entirely for us whether we do it or not. Should our action affect anyone else a quite different consideration must arise. Bentham then invokes his "greatest happiness principle". Will what we do affect others? If so, we surrender our freedom to act until we have considered the consequences. The aggregate of pains and pleasures to everyone, including ourselves, will show a net outcome one way or another. So if the pains exceed the pleasures, we should desist; if the contrary, our freedom to act is restored. As we are all equal in the exercise of our freedom, as Locke contended, the element of pain and pleasure we have in the action has the same weight in the balance as that of anyone else.

John Stuart Mill (1806-1873), coming later, was able to see the danger of Bentham's utilitarianism being accepted without qualification. The public good, in a wider sense than Bentham envisaged, had to be taken into account. Was it right morally for some who were idle to eat plentifully while others worked long hours and went hungry? No man can be an island to himself, and in the society we form for our mutual advantage we have a duty to our fellow men and women to ensure that none shall fall down and suffer for it.

Mill died just before England's empire attained its zenith. Not just a quarter of the world's atlas was painted red, but countries like China, Egypt and several in South America came under her hegemony. Such power, which was diplomatic and economic as much as imperial, had a corrupting effect – as an excess of power must – upon the Englishman's character. As a later chapter attempts to show, the Englishman changed and with the change his traditional thought was ruptured too, albeit temporarily.

English philosophers have responded to the rupture by drifting down strange paths. Perhaps philosophy had advanced as far as it could, and certainly many have said that all Western philosophy, no matter from what direction it has come, has now found itself up a *cul-de-sac*. This is scarcely surprising when many of their books are denying any point in philosophy. Nor is it particularly encouraging to prospective students when told philosophy is about language and analysis and little else. Worse still, in US universities they call such arid studies the Anglo-Saxon philosophy. Maybe one day the modern philosopher will stop writing books with titles like *Language, Truth and Logic* or *Mind, Truth and Probability* or *Mind, Language and Reality* or *Logic, Reality and Probability*, then confess he is at the end of the *cul-de-sac* and the English empiricists had said all that we need to know about political and moral principles.

These logical positivists, linguistic analysists and their associated allies may claim they have merely brought empiricism to its logical destination. What is the point of epistemology, metaphysics, theology and theories of knowledge or of logic if their propositions cannot lead to scientific proof? Yes, but the same can be said of those remaining segments of philosophy, ethics and politics. Yet to dismiss their study as equally meaningless is to rule out debate on the fundamental questions about society. Both can rely upon experience; and experience can lead to an empirical conclusion. This self-evident truth has been splendidly explored by two English thinkers in the last decades of the twentieth century, Karl Popper and Isaiah Berlin. English they are, for they settled in England and were culturally as English as King Alfred himself, although they or their fathers may have been born far away. Their books have been acclaimed, and both in the universities and beyond they have been justly honoured. In their hands the English tradition in the fields of ethics and politics has shown that a lack of proof is no bar to a meaningful study.

English philosophy has consistently radiated from the individual; in other traditions it is the Idea, Reason, Salvation, Spirit or some other nebulous notion. In deciding, therefore, the proper relationship between the state and the individual – and no fundamental question is more important in politics – the English have said firmly it is grounded on an implied contract and not on status. Both the Scots and the Continentals decided the question differently, giving them another view of how human rights are derived, as a later chapter shows. This is scarcely surprising given the origins of Anglo-Saxon society and the feudal system both on the Continent and in Scotland. So again, we come back to the importance of land tenure and its impact upon England's culture.

Chapter 6

When in Rome...

Not much imagination is needed to agree with Hobbes that life in the state of nature was "nasty, brutish and short", and our most distant forebears surrendered their unfettered freedom to form civil societies for that obvious reason. Each one evolved according to the primitive values and beliefs of its members. From one millennium to the next they have continued to evolve, stretching into every crevice of the globe. Most of these societies had no distinctive cultures to prevent them merging with neighbours to form a larger tribe, and one merger led to another. The Jutes of Kent felt able to join with the South Saxons, and together with other Saxons in due course they merged with Mercia, the Danelaw and Northumbria. Much the same happened in the rest of Europe and indeed throughout a large part of the world; and though battles between these tribal societies were fought, the subsequent union usually survived. Their unity, however, depended upon there being no distinctive differences between the cultures; and they were the embryos of the modern nation state, with its distinctions between nationality, domicile and residence.

Is there anything wrong with this diversity of cultures, each represented by a nation state? If we do not like the culture of the country that is our original domicile, we can usually change to a domicile of choice to enjoy a more agreeable way of life; and if we are disappointed by what we find, it may be feasible to move further on. The diversity becomes dangerous, though, when attempts are made to create a civil society, as may happen in the larger states, with two or more different cultural homogenities; and as readers may have gathered by now, that is the principal theme of this book.

So why is culture to the body politic what the heart is to the body itself? We noted earlier that in any civil society there has to be an allocation of rights and responsibilities, and in the modern state a large number of these are transferred from the individual to an agency of the government. Although in a democracy the allocation is made by elected politicians, they are tied by the powers they are given. These powers boil down to just two: the power to make laws and the power to impose taxes. One takes away the freedom of the people to behave as they wish, the other takes away their money. Both are handed over to the government, and a democratic government is powerless to do anything unless at least one of those two freedoms is first of all taken away. Unless one's instincts are totally authoritarian – or one is willing to be a serf – this denial of what nature has kindly bestowed is not a triviality. Both legislation and taxation are acts of coercion. Refusal to obey the law or pay a tax demand will lead inexorably (as readers have been reminded already) to a place in the dock where burglars, rapists and murderers have stood and will stand again; and persistent refusal, on matters of principle, will require another criminal to be removed to a place where even more freedom is taken away. To be logically persuaded that the law or tax was fair is not enough; in a just society we should *feel* they are fair, and without that feeling, which is decided by our emotions as well as our reason, there can be no sense of justice. Our feelings, we can be sure, flow more from our culture than from any process of ratiocination. How then can a multicultural society decide on the laws and taxes that make possible the government of a country? It can be attempted, and in Britain today that is happening, but the more it is attempted the less will people feel they live in a just society. Allow this feeling to go beyond a certain stage, and a government will find it has an ungovernable people. At best, a multicultural state will have parallel sets of laws, which in turn may require parallel courts with different procedures. Indeed Britain has set a precedent in that direction already. Some years ago Parliament passed a law requiring every motor-cyclist to wear a protective helmet. This made it a crime not to protect oneself from an injury, a new principle. Hitherto the liberal doctrine had prevailed, that we could behave as we liked provided we did nothing to annoy anyone else. But Sikhs coming to Britain and wishing to ride motor bicycles raised a protest. Their turbans were a sign of manhood, and part of their culture, and helmets could not fit on top of them. So Parliament duly obliged by passing a further Act allowing Sikhs to be above that particular law. This privilege has done no harm; we are unlikely to see swarms of helmetless Sikhs careering through our towns exciting indignation against such favouritism. Nevertheless, the precedent could become the thin end of a very big wedge, that could stretch the nation's toleration too far For the English have always tolerated ideas, opinions and the freedom to express them, however forthright, whimsical or bizarre; but they do not happily tolerate special privileges.

Beside me is a leaflet advertising a rally in Trafalgar Square, which is reproduced on the next page. It was to be "against Freedom and Democracy". To whet the appetite, there is on the back the essence of the argument. Britain has become overwhelmed by family breakdown, child abuse, homosexuality, drug addiction and so on a democratic government panders to the morals of those who do not know how to behave. That particular rally was held in 1995 and it was far from being the last of its kind. Activities like this must be having a cumulative effect, and indeed the message is very plausible. My God! some people may say, they are right. Then comes the punchline. "Britain is no place for our families – we must have Moslem laws."

In an English monocultural society, toleration is part of the culture, and rallies in Trafalgar Square can be allowed every day to denounce what is wrong. But what these fundamentalists want is another parliament, different courts and another legal system, founded upon another culture. In a word, they want to

LAST YEAR THE INTERNATIONAL MUSLIM KHILAFAH CONFERENCE ROCKED THE WORLD; THIS YEAR, THE VOICE OF ISLAM WILL SHAKE THE VERY FOUNDATIONS OF WESTERN CIVILISATION...

RALLY FOR
ISLAM

Reject the evils of freedom and democracy, the pillars of the west!
Support Islam...the Supreme Ideology

- Bosnia...the reality of western democratic failure and hypocrisy in the world!
- New world order is an order of death, disease, rape and destruction!
- Endemic crime, homosexuality, poverty, family breakdown, drug and alcohol abuse shows freedom and democracy just aren't working
- Islam...the system of the Creator, the medicine for the diseases of freedom and democracy

The world needs change..it needs Islam..it needs Khilafah, the Islamic ruling system!

Speakers include ● Omar Bakri Mohammed ● Farid Kassim Jamal Harwood ● Abdul Wajid

TRAFALGAR SQUARE
3PM
13 AUGUST '95

Islam...The Future

The Rally for Islam is not an invitation to a religion, it is a call to the supreme ideology...the system of the Creator...Islam! The world needs Islam, Britain needs Islam. Urban riots, suicides, alcoholism, family breakdowns, child abuse, homosexuality, drug addiction, racism, poverty, unemployment and general lawlessness all bare testimony that the western secular way of life just isn't working. Life is in a constant state of flux. Nobody trusts anybody. The escapism of nintendo, the national lottery, sports, pop music, partying and raving has become a way of life.

Escaping from what? The establishment wants to keep people drugged up with mindless, irrelevant pastimes; to stop them from thinking about the really important questions about life - it's meaning and purpose. The meaning of life has been reduced to a Monty Python joke.

The portrayal of Islam as a fanatic rag-tag terrorist system is part of this effort to keep people mindless. This is because Islam's central theme is to get people thinking and face the reality of our existence. Contemplating that reality with intellect and sincerity will inevitably lead all to the conclusion that there is a Creator. The Creator did not leave humanity floating into anarchy, as western ideology has left it. He communicated with humans via Prophets, each endowed with miracles. The final Prophet was Muhammad (peace be upon him). His miracle is the Qur'an - it is with us today. Islam is the way of life ordained by the Creator. It's way is one of human control and responsibility. It provides a complete system for all human relations. It is tried and tested - and worked; providing tranquillity for all who lived under it's system - the Khilafah system.

On Sunday 13th August 1995 in Trafalgar Square we will be addressing these issues. Further, we will not only be demonstrating the intellectual superiority of the Islamic creed but also showing the superiority of the Islamic way of life. Every government in the Muslim world, yes every government (including Iraq, Saudi Arabia, Iran, Pakistan and Sudan), are inventions of the west. They do not represent Islamic ruling. That ruling is the Khilafah system... and it's coming soon to sweep away the shallow, mindless and crime-ridden way of life the world is imprisoned by these days.

Rally for Islam at Trafalgar Square on 13 August '95 !

For further information contact, London 01712817124, 01819980868, 0956212455, Newcastle 01914561796, Cardiff 01222457356, Bradford 0374296975, Sheffield 01142796219, Birmingham 01213563415, Manchester 0831310047

Beware of false cancellations, call 0956 212 455 (24 Hours)

live in a multicultural society. Perhaps if thieving hands were chopped off, adulterers stoned to death and drunkards languished in a solitary cell for a while, the English who survived the regime might sleep more peacefully, but they would be living in a country no longer England.

In fairness to those fundamentalists, they liken their position to other fundamentalists in England, the Orthodox Jews. They have their own laws in the Talmud and their own courts in the BethDin. There is, though, a difference. The laws they apply are about domestic disputes and do not touch the fabric of English society. As these issues are private, they can be heard in private, so that most people may never have heard of BethDin or what it does. The differences between the Talmudic laws and those of England apparently cause no conflict and so need be of no concern to anyone outside the Jewish community.

For centuries it was seldom deemed necessary to add to the Statute Book. The concept of the rule of law supplemented by a body of evolving common law was enough to regulate a monocultural society. Even the advent of the financial revolution that followed the Act of Settlement in which bankers' paper took the place of the monarch's coinage, gave Parliament little work to do. Both the rule of law and the ethos of individualism were constraints upon the state. It is true that in the predominantly agrarian society that existed until the Industrial Revolution, most people lived in small communities, where self-interest, if no other reason, persuaded them to treat their neighbours as they themselves would wish to be be treated. In those communities an Englishman's word had to be his bond. Yet on the Continent, equally agrarian, there were endless changes in the regulation of people's lives. Some may attribute this to the fickle minds of authoritarian rulers. Another, and perhaps more likely, explanation is that on the Continent they had never responded to the individualist belief that laws which take away people's freedom were only justified if they protected one of what Bastiat called the three gifts of God, life, liberty and property.

But a change has come upon England. Today no constraints of that kind curb the zeal of the race relations industry. To maintain the number of jobs it provides, a cynic may be justified in thinking, the public – or more specifically the government – has to be persuaded that racial prejudice is not in decline but becoming worse. Their accusing finger points at any institution susceptible to moral blackmail. The murder of one boy, evil though it undoubtedly was, has given the industry a feast of opportunities. As a result a policeman heard to ask for a cup of black coffee in his canteen now has to face disciplinary proceedings. Teachers speak of being terrorised into turning a Nelsonian eye upon an Asian or black pupil whose behaviour would bring certain punishment for a pupil with a white skin. Employers complain they face the charge of racial discrimination so readily that they are forced to be prejudiced against employees who are white. Nor should we overlook what is happening in some of the erstwhile polytechnics, now universities, where standards are somewhat below mediocre. A mature student, defined as anyone over 21 years old, may be admitted without any GCSEs let alone an A level, and once enrolled need attend lectures and submit essays no more than he or she feels inclined. Then racial discrimination takes a turn. Although every student will be awarded some sort of degree, for otherwise the university may forego its money, the wholly hopeless examinee who gets a third can play the race card, if racially qualified to do so, and be assured of something more respectable. One university lecturer is known to me to have left a university because of this racial prejudice.

Abuses such as these occur every day in every segment of English life when races now mix together, as they must in a multiracial society. Far from seeing wrong in all forms of racial prejudice, the race relations industry is actively promoting further abuse by what it says and does, not least of all by its veiled threats of "more must be done" and with its demand for positive discrimination. Indeed, more must be done, if our multiracial society is to succeed. The harmony we desire will not come if this form of racial prejudice stirs a reaction by its victims who will feel that not only they but their country and its culture is under attack. We can only speculate about what form the reaction will take.

It is English toleration that has enabled over five million immigrants and their descendants to comprise a tenth of the country's population, and in the conurbations where they have mostly come, sometimes a third or more of the population. Other nations would have behaved differently to the threat to jobs, wages and housing. Yet even in the schools where over twenty different languages may be spoken, and the teaching is handicapped, neither the parents nor the teachers threaten to raise a voice in protest. The Inner London Education Authority stated in 1986 that there were 161 different languages spoken in its schools; and it is believed the number has now reached about 200.

Toleration is a priceless ingredient of the nation's culture. But to force English chief constables, teachers, academics, employers and others to be racially prejudiced against the English in their charge does little to achieve true racial equality. But how can there be a truly multiracial society without racial equality? Better surely to remove as speedily as is practical the inequalities suffered by the minorities without creating resentment by the majority. Resentment can turn nasty, surging up in unexpected places, and it is now much more widespread than many people reckon. It is strongest not among the rich and influential but among the weak and the poor, for they are always the ones on whom injustice bears most heavily. And when the burden of injustice becomes too great history tells that it is the weak who resort to violence. They are weak in the sense that they feel powerless to redress their wrongs by other means but they may have strength enough to rise up and force a riot. It is an urgent duty to prevent this resentment from growing until it is out of control.

A vicious circle is so easily created. An aggressively prejudiced minority of white people – and no one denies that such a minority exists – creates fear and defensiveness in the people who are the object of its hatred. This quickly leads to a ghetto mentality and to a separation of racial groups with each side claiming moral superiority over the other. Such a situation is ripe for political exploitation and exploited it has certainly been It can be corrected only by a genuinely tolerant environment in which the extremists of both sides are exposed and denounced, the Trotskyites along with the neo-Nazis. For in the harm they do to the cause of racial integration and harmony there is little to choose between them.

Another threat to England's unity of culture comes in a variety of ways from the European Union. The concept of the rule of law is unknown on the Continent, for as we have noted the term is interpreted quite differently in their courts. The writ of *habeas corpus* and trial by jury are both scarcely known outside the English-speaking world, and both are under threat by amendments to the Treaty of Rome.

The ethos of individualism is almost beyond comprehension in the institutions of the EU, so that the notion there is an implied contract between the state and the individual has never been theirs. The fundamental freedoms that uphold the principle of toleration are throughout Europe conferred by a benign state and not seen as the individual's birthright, inherited from time immemorial. As to the influence of empiricism it has no followers across the Channel. That each of the four ingredients of England's culture is either unknown or unaccepted in nearly all the rest of the EU will make it difficult for the English people to be comfortable in its bosom, unless of course they reject the culture that has made them what they are.

As a country's culture determines how its people behave, no two countries in the world have quite the same collection of laws or fiscal systems, not even England and Scotland. This explains why states that embrace two cultures are now in various stages of disintegration. Unless one is of the same culture as the country itself, it naturally goes against the grain to respect, even accept, all its laws. which is why a multicultural society can never enjoy a sense of unity. It is also a contradiction in terms. When the Society of Boilermakers begins to admit members who cannot make boilers and are not really interested in how they are made, but are happy to join the Society because they enjoy the jolly evenings they have, the Society ceases to be what it purports to be. So, too, with England; immigrants ought to be welcomed if they feel able to accept the culture that has made England what she is. But England ceases to be the land of the English if immigrants want to stay, determined not to shed the core values and beliefs which belong to another country and are radically different from those of the English. Of course, the British did exactly that in creating their Empire, but two wrongs never make a right.

It was also another wrong when the early immigrants to North America behaved as they did to the indigenous Indians. The latter's belief that the land was the private property of no man and a life of hunter-gathering was the basis of an economy could not be reconciled with what the new Americans had in mind to do. That a terrible injustice was done is beyond dispute, but it shows once again that when two cultures clash, one must overide the other. The clash resolved, no part of the world has taken up the challenge of multiracialism more successfully than the United States. Her Founding Fathers, WASPs to a man, enshrined the Anglo-Saxon belief in toleration in the Declaration of Independence, and put it into practice. When, decades later, wave upon wave of immigrants came from many different cultures, they were welcomed, but with a proviso. They had to turn their backs upon the values and beliefs that had regulated the governance of their homelands. They were to be out-and-out Americans or nothing. They had to learn the English language, and accept another citizenship. They were told of the constitution and what it meant. They had to salute the Stars and Stripes. Uncle Sam, they were told, is your uncle too; and, gee, you've gotta stick to the family rules. It worked. Monoculturalism was imposed upon multiracialism, and a great nation entered the twentieth century. It is true that in more recent years concessions have been made to the Hispanics, largely because most of them arrived illegally and it has been impractical to do otherwise. But there has been resentment by anglophone Americans, evident in polls in the states where Hispanics have mainly gone.

To speak of the United States as a multicultural community is absurd. In both the United States and Canada there remain many indigenous Native Americans; their culture is so different that it is difficult to find a single meeting-point. One is basically Anglo-Saxon, the other similar to that of many indigenous peoples in South America and a large part of Africa before colonisation, as well as the Australian Aborigines. The latter all believe in a communistic society based upon the tribe. Nature and a deity are at one, and the notion therefore that an individual can legally be the owner of nature, in the form of some acres of land, is quite beyond their comprehension. Their pantheism enables them to trust nature to provide the needs of the tribe, so that they can hope to lead a life in accordance with nature. There is, though, a limit to what nature can supply, and this means the tribe cannot settle on one site, but must become nomadic over a wide area.

The democratic principle that a majority can decide how a minority should behave is also strange to them. Instead, when an important decision has to be made by the tribe, its members will gather round the Chief and continue to debate the issue until the Chief concludes that a consensus has been reached. As for the rest of Western civilisation, the thousands of laws and regulations, the ever-growing edifice of bureaucracy, the millions of people tearing around in cars or solemnly sitting for hours cooped up in an office gazing at an electronic screen or standing monotonously beside an assembly line or flying up in the air for thousands of miles for a holiday away from it all, all that and much else must convince the Indians that the white man is quite mad; and perhaps they know the old adage about whom the gods wish to destroy. In short, the native Americans, like the Aborigines, must either be assimilated or live in a self-contained society according to a different culture. To describe that second option there is, of course, a word in Afrikaans.

The US policy on immigration was founded upon the simple proposition that an immigrant arrives with one of two motives. He may come because he likes what he has heard about the country, and is willing to accept its culture; or he may come to make money out of its people, which he may or may not remit to his homeland. That may not be a polite way of describing what is sometimes called an economic immigrant, but it states in plain words what is surely reality. The gulf between them is wide: the first is welcomed and the door is flung open, whatever their race or homeland may be, because they are going to be American. As for the other, why it seems not unreasonable for him to be told the old adage about what one should do when one goes to Rome. Those who advocate making England into a multicultural society have failed so far to explain why the same principle should not apply to their own country.

But how can he "do as the Romans" when so much is being done to accentuate his sense of alienation? Of course, it suits the neo-Nazi and the extremist on the far Left since they can best achieve their aims in a divided society. The *provocateurs* in the Communist movement have their useful idiots, as Lenin called them, who are much more dangerous since their influence enters the daily life of the thousands of blacks and Asians who already feel discontented with life in Britain. Circulating among teachers, social workers, journalists and even the police, these useful idiots are doing the work Lenin predicted they would do in deepening the divisions of society. The bodies of which they are a part are also gradually becoming imbued with a form of institutional racialism. These bodies interpret racism in only one way, an injury of some kind to a black or Asian. When precisely the same things are said or done to a white person, solely on account of the colour of their skin, it also is, in any reasonable mind, an act of racism. A racial attack upon someone of the indigenous majority by someone of an ethnic minority that feels oppressed can be explicable, and to that extent less heinous, but if we are to say racisim is wrong, the word ought to cover all its forms.

In the town I have known since childhood, where several thousands of immigrant origin have come to live, the police have indeed become institutionally racist. It is common knowledge that, as often as about once a week, white boys are attacked by black ones. When the white boys are seriously injured, and they have been taken to hospital, and the police are called, the response is always the same. "You don't want to press charges, do you?" the complainant, usually a parent, will be told, and the police will insist the attack was not racist because the victim was not black. When the complaint is taken further, the answer has been on several occasions that a letter can be sent to the Home Secretary. Other police forces are reported to act in the same way, so it looks as if it is becoming a general policy.

However, we might ask ourselves why it is that these attacks now endemic in our inner city areas, should be committed by the present generation when the same kind of violence was seldom caused by their fathers when they were the same age. Something must have effected this change for the worse. It could be a reaction to the hatred generated by the neo-Nazis, but their numbers have been on the wane throughout this time, and since the end of the National Front their activities have been minimal. There are a few other extreme groups calling themselves chapters, but Special Branch has been reported as stating that membership is so small that their influence can be of little consequence. We could turn to their competitors, the militant Left, but they have been on the wane, too. What has not decreased is the number of useful idiots, their role endorsed by national policy.

By promoting racial consciousness they have created a natural demand for a sub-culture among the ethnic minorities. It has taken two forms, and both have involved commercial interests, one of which is making a great deal of money. Rap music has become a very profitable industry and it is estimated that hundreds of thousands of pounds are being made by the many musicians, lyricists, singers and producers of disks and gigs. The words that thunder through the microphone are of a new genre. "It is good to make a white girl have a baby: and you don't have to marry her." That may not be urging girls to be raped, but it is scarcely good ethics, and it is plainly racist. Not all are about hate and violence, but the general tenor, spiced with expletives, is hard and harsh, and the music itself equally so. This being their choice, it can do nothing to fortify their better nature or uplift their spirits, and one may wonder what the cumulative effect must be in changing the way many young blacks see themselves and the milieu in which they live.

Publishers supplying demand in the sub culture will not make so much money, but that may be no measure of the mischief they are making. Books and magazines are coming out to promote an alternative culture, much of it based upon a strange interpretation of history. The educationalists who decree how history is to be taught have a charge to answer.

The story of England was once learnt in every school in the country and schools in other countries count it as a duty to teach their own history. A whole generation, and some say it is two generations, has been denied knowledge about itself. This denial reaches to the universities. Writing in the *Oxford Magazine* in October 1998, Dr John Maddicott said a student could obtain an honours degree in history without knowing anything about Magna Carta, the Black Death, the Reformation, the Glorious Revolution or the Reform Bill of 1832. As these are the most significant landmarks in England's story since the time of the Conquest, it is a sorry indictment by a distinguished historian. Oxford is not alone, for the controversy that followed his revelation showed that only one or two seats of learning taught English history in what was once considered the only appropriate way. If graduates in history are not to know what shaped England's course and made her people what they are today, what hope is there for the rest of us? One of the reasons for this denial of knowledge is that Marxists have entered the field and by an emphasis upon certain chapters of social and economic history have given themselves the opportunity to interpret events in a manner favourable to their cause. Having myself heard one of these lectures, I can vouch for the persuasive effect it had upon the audience. The question remains, how do we know the path we are on, unless we know how we came to be where we are?

The vacuum created by the educational policy-makers is being filled in the towns where there are ethnic minorities, and black people in particular have available to them no shortage of history books written especially for them. Roy Kerridge in the *Story of Black History*[1] has revealed what these books are about. Kerridge was prompted to write about black history after seeing a display of books in Willesden Green public library. Black civilisation, we are told, existed long before the Greeks, whose philosophers such as Plato and Aristotle shamelessly plagiarised the far greater thinkers of Africa. Cleopatra was black, so was Beethoven and many other geniuses. Blacks were made superior to whites by nature since they are "sun people", carefree and mentally well-adjusted, while whites are condemned to be "ice people", therefore cold-hearted and psychologically repressed, a state of mind that induces them to be repressive of others. The English, needless to say, poor things, are ice people, but not the Scots, for they were once blacks out of Africa.

This sort of education for the blacks is not just to be found in public libraries paid for by the British taxpayer; the print runs for these books are quite considerable and they are sold in numerous shops catering specially for blacks. How many thousands have read them no one knows, but their readers, denied knowledge of their adopted country when at school, have no reason to question what they read in these books. Far from being assimilated and absorbed into one society, they are made to feel alienated; and if as a result they are full of hate, the blame does not rest on them. Kerridge is well known for his fervent desire to improve race relations; and not surprisingly his book is also a plea for history to be taught in our schools objectively and fairly, lest good relations between black and white are put in still greater peril.

Perhaps it is unnecessary to add that to love a country, especially a new homeland, is impossible, unless one knows about

[1] Roy Kerridge, *The Story of Black History*; The Claridge Press, 1998.

its people and their history and about its institutions and how they have come to be as they are. To deny an immigrant that knowledge is bad enough; to deny it to the natives is likely to make them nationalistic, and therefore assertive, instead of patriots who love all homelands. But against whom will the natives be assertive? It is a question that the race relations industry might ponder.

Chapter 7

The Imperial Interlude

Since as many sons, and daughters too, set off from the homesteads of Scotland, Wales and Ireland to build an empire as did from England, it was always a British Empire. In fact, wherever traders, merchants, missionaries, soldiers and administrators went to change the lives of hundreds of millions of people in other parts of the world, the English were generally in a minority. The fathers, mothers, brothers and sisters who stayed behind, proud of their kin, gloried in the news of the imperial venture; and as most families could claim at least a cousin in the empire, the aggregated pride of the British swelled with every advance among those deemed to be lesser mortals. More than any other factor it welded the four nations into what was claimed to be a single British nation. And so long as the British Empire gave them that sense of pride, the Scots, Welsh, even many Irish, were content to call themselves British. One should never generalise about the Irish, though: Wolf Tone and his United Irishmen were around at the genesis of empire, the Fenians at its zenith, and the IRA when the nemesis began, but throughout those years their fellow countrymen (and the Anglo-Irish insisted they were as much Irish as the rest, and behaved rather more so) were in the forefront of the Empire's advance, notably in the ranks of the conquering armies. Indeed, the Irish did rather more than their fair share of the vanquishing; and one, Charles Napier, whose soldiers had stood guard over colonies in four continents and ended his military career in his sixties by annexing the Sind, declared his policy to be "first thrash em hard, then treat em kindly," just as gamekeepers trained their gundogs.

Before the Empire became a force in the world, observers from abroad recorded little sense of one nation: Britain and British were words seldom heard. Until the Act of Union in 1800, Ireland had her own House of Commons and administration in Dublin, allowing her to feel semi-detached, and whilst Wales was constitutionally one with England, the central government hardly touched the everyday life of the Welsh, and ever since a Welshman took the English throne, there was really nothing to stir a grievance. Besides, being overwhelmingly Protestant, they had every reason to appreciate the protection of the English umbrella from repeated threats of invasion by Catholic Spain or France; and when Napoleon's troops landed on Pembrokeshire, it was the womenfolk in frightening attire who chased them back to the boats. Only by the King of Scotland coming to Westminster to take England's throne was the other Act of Union accepted, and we might remember it was as late as 1745 that a Scots force invaded England, reaching her very heart in Derbyshire.

To mock Britain's role in the imperial interlude, much has been said and written on the stage and screen, in countless histories, biographies and even novels; and lessons in school and lectures in universities have been given to belittle past heroes. The Empire changed the English. They became in their nature and behaviour a different people, albeit temporarily. Now, the Empire gone, there is ample evidence that the English are going back to being and behaving as in their past.

Power, we are often told, has a corrupting effect. Lord Acton's famous dictum is generally misunderstood, for it is rarely quoted in its context. It was written in 1857 in a letter to Mantell Creighton, the Bishop of London, after Acton had read his *History of the Papacy*. "I cannot accept," Lord Acton wrote, "your canon that we are to judge pope and king unlike other men, with a favourable presumption that they did no wrong. If there was any presumption, it is the other way, against the holders of power. Historic responsibility has to make up for that want of legal responsibility. Power tends to corrupt, and absolute power corrupts absolutely. Great men are almost always bad men, even when they exercise influence and not authority."

The corruption of the British, and hence the English character, was marked particularly, it was said, among the less well educated, the clerks, shop keepers, commercial travellers and others whose rising standard of living owed much to the Empire. When Mr Cook's travel agency began its famous tours, many thousands of these representatives of England were able to afford a visit to France and other countries in Europe. Not deigning to speak more of a foreigner's tongue than they wished, a not untypical comment was often heard: "If you shout loud enough at em, they will understand," to which might be added "they only want our money, don't they?" which came to be quite true. *Punch* had a cartoon depicting an irate Cook's tourist threatening a French café proprietor, "I will write to *The Times* about you," with the caption "The Englishman's Ultimate Threat". Even in the last years of the Raj, when serving in India, I remember how Tommy Atkins still treated the Indian people, or at least those he encountered, with the same ill-regard. The attitude was to be expected: a pride of nationhood lifted up the English to let them look down upon the rest of the human race – after all, in terms of power they had become superior. Not just the Cook's tourists and the lower ranks of the military acquired this arrogance; all England shared in the pride that swelled into various degrees of jingoism. Uninhibited in the sing-songs heard in the music halls and the public bars on a Saturday night, and more sophisticated in the salons of Mayfair and at country house dinner parties, a self-assured nation knew greatness had been thrust upon it. Great Britain had an historic role to bring peace and good government to the lesser peoples of the world. There was indeed much truth in what they were saying: peace did come to countless millions and so did good government. Only a few dissented, like John Stuart Mill. "Good government," he wrote, "is no substitute for self-government," and several decades were to pass before his words were echoed by many others.

Although the Empire, strictly speaking, began long before Victoria's reign, it had been incidental to the lives of most of the English: a few sought their fortune in the plantations of the West Indies and North America or went off to join the East India Company, and still fewer went willingly to uncongenial climates elsewhere, whilst it was in hundreds rather than thousands that they sailed even more unwillingly to the penal settlements. Not until the end of the eighteenth century, with the advent of the Industrial Revolution, did the interest in an Empire grow. A passage to India was still for the wayward son hoping to return as a rich nabob, and the West Indies in the minds of many were only fit for pirates and the decadent, while to the North American colonies the annual migration was seldom more than a few hundreds. It was not only Edmund Burke who questioned the value of an empire; public opinion was indifferent; at best it was for younger sons made landless by primogeniture.

In short, the English character was still unaffected: and in essentials unchanged from what it was in Anglo-Saxon times. England was still predominantly an agrarian nation, overwhelmingly dependent for its income on what came from the land, and the principles that knitted society together were the same as they had been for a thousand years. To have land mattered: to win it was a mark of social and political as well as economic significance. The loss of land was more than a misfortune: with rank and status also lost, the dispossessed suffered a humbler life in the squalor of a town or, as many did, with bowed head quit the neighbourhood to live in penury as an agricultural labourer far from his roots. The merchant families were primarily living in London or in ports like Bristol and Liverpool; the professional classes were few and members of the armed forces still fewer. Agriculture and everything that went with it was the English interest. In the market towns – and all towns had a market necessarily – the talk was of farming and its fortunes. As the farmers circulated around the streets on market day, they were canvassed for their views about the growing crops and the effect of last week's weather, not for reasons of courtesy, for it was intelligence about the future welfare of everyone living in the town. Once the shopkeepers prospered it was their ambition to aspire to a farm of their own. Land gave status, respectability and the franchise. For land-owning farmers to have the vote was considered a quite logical privilege: they had a stake in the country's fortunes: and their fortunes, were the ones upon which the rest of the population was dependent. The mainspring of the nation's wealth in their hands and their status in society both coveted and unquestioned, the assumption followed that they were fit and proper persons to whom matters of government could safely be left. Even locally, the magistracy and grand juries were filled almost exclusively from their ranks.

The imperial interlude changed that; for it was also the period when the majority of the English became divorced from the very system of land tenure that had done so much to create Englishness. Of the English that stayed at home, they moved in their droves to the new towns to labour for another class of employer and to live as tenants in the rows of terraces built around the mills, mines, foundries and factories. The agricultural labourers may have only left their hovels, but the Industrial Revolution brought to an end the independence of countless thousands of craftsmen, such as weavers, spinners, wheelwrights, tanners, carriers and many others, who had hitherto earned a living in country districts. self-employed and in their own cottages and plot of land where they grew much of their own food.

The spirit of individualism survived in the countryside among the farmers or at least those who owned their own land and were free of debt or mortgages. Such farmers are rare today, for agricultural policy has driven them to expand their output and the expansion has committed them to bank managers and other mortgagees. It was a different story when the fortunes of agriculture were seen to be less certain. The uncertainty, though, made the yeoman even more of an individualist. Come sickness or misfortune, he had to stand on his own two feet, and only in the short-term would his neighbours be able to come to his aid. Although a large proportion of the farmers had by then become tenants of large estates, their status had remained virtually unchanged. Provided the rent was paid, their occupation was generally secure; and the evidence suggests that even if their rent was not paid for some good reason, it was rare for them to be evicted. They were yeomen *de facto*.

Now another kind of yeomanry is evolving. More English people own their own homes with gardens than ever before; the number increases daily. In no other country outside the English-speaking-world is the proportion of freeholders so high; and in the US, Canada, Australia and New Zealand where land is much cheaper and the opportunity to build one's home is so much easier, the proportion is not substantially greater. True, most of the English are burdened by a mortgage. The fact that there are millions willing to commit much of their income to the purchase of a home instead of spending their money on the comforts and luxuries of life serves to show the innate desire to have control over their own bit of England, and the instinct seems as great as it was among their distant ancestors centuries ago.

One of the most popular acts of any British government in the last half-century has been the decision to require local authorities to sell their council houses to the tenants who wanted to buy them. The response has been amazing: in their hundreds of thousands the tenants queued up to buy. Whole roads became owner-occupied. Now in the estates anyone can tell which is still tenanted and which has become the property of a freeholder. The gardens, especially, are significant. They signify how their owners have inherited a love of cultivation. The Welsh and Scots may not wish it to be said, but the gardens of their erstwhile council houses seldom look quite the same as the English.

The next chapter speaks of the electronic age. The revolution that began in the last years of the twentieth century will do more than anything else to bring a yeomanry back to England.

About one-third of the work now done in our cities and conurbations will be capable of being performed electronically; whether it is done within the home or not will be of no moment. As both the employed and the self-employed will be able to work just as well at home as in some office or factory, it seems probable that most will choose to do so at home. Some jobs may require some days in attendance elsewhere as is the case now with many teleworkers, but a journey on those days of fifty or sixty miles may be a tolerable inconvenience. The electronic revolution will thus liberate millions: they will be free to live and work in the countryside instead of those congested urban areas that are becoming steadily less congenial for most people. Even if a majority stay behind, there will still be something of an exodus which will make the conurbations even less amenable and even less of a place to bring up children. The inner cities especially will sink in a downward spiral; as families in well-paid employment move out, so an underclass will increase its proportion of the population, and with it more vandalism, graffiti, drugs, theft and the rest of the long catalogue of crime that makes the cities, once defined as the centres of civilisation, scenes of uncivilised living. The underclass and the computer illiterate, may not quite be one and the same, but there will be a distinctive correlation. The electronically literate will be well-paid; and the nation's majority will be that too. As millions take advantage of the new freedom, we can envisage a mass migration to England's more rural areas. The countryside will no doubt suffer by the invasion, but many of the new owner-occupiers may aspire to the rural idyll. Among those who have made the move already thousands have discovered a satisfying antidote to their tired eyes behind a screen in an occupation so divorced from nature. It is to go out into the fresh air, cultivate a smallholding with perhaps a few hens and perhaps a goat, as well as grow their own vegetables and pick plums and apples from their own trees. It is a re-creation indeed. If only a small proportion of the ten million able to make the move actually do so and pursue that recreational activity, there will be numerically more yeomen of England than ever before. England's individualism will be reborn. With the dark satanic mills gone, even William Blake's vision may be on the way.

An earlier chapter has shown how the Anglo-Saxon system of land tenure enhanced the spirit of individualism, until the days of empire began, which came almost simultaneously with the Agricultural Revolution. In farming especially there is a correlation between money borrowed and time spent worrying. Some three decades in the mid-nineteenth century the farming community prospered and its profits flowed in to build the new mills, mines, factories and warehouses. By today's standards the farms were mere smallholdings. They were still, throughout most of the middle and southern England, usually about forty acres, although they might be larger in areas where soil, climate and terrain made the land unsuitable for arable crops. Even the home farms, which larger landowners retained in their possession for domestic needs, were much the same size. To preside over one of these holdings was to enjoy a degree of security denied to nearly everyone else. Although there were times of terrible social and civil upheaval, as in the Wars of the Roses and the Civil War, the chance of an army, which might consist of no more than a few thousand men, actually looting the barns and slaughtering the stock was never very great. Gray's *Elegy* could truthfully speak of "the even tenor of their lives". In a society where rustlers, arsonists and burglars went to the gallows they could feel safe in homesteads of their own. And outside there was a garden, orchard and fields that provided the most essential of all material needs. Hens fluttering about the yard, fruit and vegetables at hand, a pig or two in the sty, cows fed on hay from the meadow provided milk, butter and cheese. Game might be sacrosanct, but there were usually rabbits to net, with wheat and oats for the miller to grind into flour or meal. For fuel there was wood from the copse, and a horse in the stable for transport. Of course, dark clouds often passed over their lives; as muscles weakened in declining years, and the effort required to plough an acre a day or garner the crops in the heat of the sun may have made them ponder the price of independence. If the civil wars passed them by, the Conquest, the Black Death, the expansion of the monastery lands and their subsequent dissolution had far-reaching effects from which few could escape: still given that the portrait stretches over a thousand years, it can be said the city merchants and others unconnected to the land may have had more of the luxuries of life, but over the years their fortunes would vacillate like mercury, whereas the yeoman, who remained in good health and worked hard, could usually hand over to a son the property with its status for him to enjoy as he had in his turn. The security turned on their independence, one went with the other; and striding across the bit of England that was theirs to command as "masters of all they surveyed", decreeing what each field should grow and which animal should live or die – all this made them different men from what he would otherwise have been. Not for nothing were they personalised as John Bull, sturdy, self-reliant and sanguinary-minded, contemptuous of idlers, wasters and beggars.

A man's chosen recreation is no bad indicator of his inner self. Until the nineteenth century, there was little evidence of any team spirit and the inclination towards cricket or football was rarely evident. Neither gained popularity until the advent of the major and now famous public schools, whose numbers increased when parents departed for the Empire. Several of them evolved out of local grammar schools and such games as they had played in the past tended to be individualistic; fighting in one form or another was considered a useful outlet for surplus energy, and it rid the young gentleman of his atavistic instincts. Team games came in with the Empire and some might say they are going out with its dissolution. Both football and cricket are losing the team spirit of yesterday, with players becoming evermore individualistic as they play to the terraces. An adroit goal scored by a player no longer has his opponent pat him on the back; instead there's a grimace or a cry of "foul". Referees get spat upon and opponents jostled. In the last days of the Empire, every player was paid exactly the same, £8 a week, until the

1940s when it was doubled to £16; and equality of pay empha-sised that each man was an equal in the team. Now players with pop appeal are among the top earners of society; and one, according to newspaper reports, received more than a million pounds for not playing for England, the money coming from newspaper articles and television chat shows. This individual-ism seems to be taking us back to the eighteenth century. On the cricket field football's ethos is catching on.

Croquet and real tennis were well established in the 1700s. Scotland's golf, although equally individualistic, had yet to be introduced. Less refined and much more painful was shinsticks, which with wrestling was especially popular in country areas. In the towns, cockfighting pits drew large crowds. The Turf, yet to be regulated, drew a motley mixture of pickpockets and other rogues to mingle among their affluent victims. As the majority of the nation still lived in the countryside, it is not surprising that fieldsports were the predominant recreation of those of the nation with time for leisure; and which ever form they take, they are highly individualistic. One field sport, fishing, is said to gain tens of thousands of new participants every year, becoming as popular as it was in pre-imperial times.

Another index of character is support, or lack of it, for the arts. Considering the size of England's population and how small the proportion that lived in the metropolis or the larger towns, the support for the theatre and the opera house was remarkable, particularly the former. The ratio of theatres to people in London was about three times greater than what it is today; and in the eighteenth century there were no railways or motorways to bring thousands every evening to see a perfor-mance as they can do now. Long before Shakespeare, the English were stage-struck; in their nature there is a thespian streak and dressing up for charades, masques, fancy dress dances and amateur dramatics had an instinctive appeal, not shared by the dour Scots or more demure Welsh, nor indeed does it seem quite so apparent anywhere else in the world. The masques of Vauxhall and elsewhere ended with the Regency;

David Garrick had no great successor; and in Victoria's reign to be an actor was no longer an entrée to what came to be called good society; few new plays came after Sheridan, and theatres themselves saw smaller audiences. What a renaissance in the last half of the twentieth century! Actors are celebrities and theatres full once more.

Why is this? The stage is hardly a career for the inhibited, the self-conscious, the pompous or disciplined conformist. As Ethel Barrymore almost said, "the actor ought to have the looks of Adonis, the memory of Macauley, the grace of a gazelle, as well as the skin of a rhinoceros, the self-worth of a Narcissus and the individualism of an egocentric," The merchant adventurers, the explorers, undoubtedly the buccaneers and the others who set off originally to trade or conquer must have had most of those thespian qualities. The same could never be said of the products of the public schools who later went out to administer the new Empire or who stayed at home conscious of Great Britain's superiority, an attitude that permeated down to the humblest of the nation as they laboured under the eye of the overseer in the mills and foundries.

An indicator of a person's character is his clothes, and so it must be of a nation's when fashions change. Almost as soon as Queen Victoria was crowned, a major change came over what nowadays is called the dress code. Out went gaiety, exuberance and individuality, and in came uniformity: drab coats became ubiquitous. Whilst it is true that a similar change came to most of western Europe and to most of the English-speaking world, there was a distinction between the two. In Britain, and especially England, there was a far greater degree of uniformity, and in most of western Europe the gay colours of traditional dresses were still to be seen.

In the advance to general dullness, anyone out of step was not just frowned upon, but positively shunned. To dress incorrectly was "not done". Whether one's sleeve had four buttons or three was not a matter of sartorial taste: it determined whether you were a gentleman or a bounder. Was all this no more than the vanity and vagary of fashion that happened to coincide with the coming and going of the Empire, or does it point to some real connection between the two?

The Empire gave the British pride, self-esteem and a fair touch of arrogance. These are the feelings of a recruit to the Brigade of Guards, when once accepted by his comrades as one of them. An *esprit de corps* moulds the young soldier's mindset, he knows he is letting down the regiment – and therefore everyone else in it including himself – if he comports himself differently from others. To share with them that pride, self-esteem and a touch of arrogance, it is necessary to think and act as they do. Even in the shipyards or in the docks, down the mines or in the mills and sweatshops of the East End, no matter the poverty or squalor of their lives, the people were conscious of belonging to a nation superior to any other. Theirs was the spirit of a famous regiment; and whatever the walk of life, people conformed to those around them.

Both music and poetry also went into decline with the rise of the Empire. Most country towns of any size used to have their chamber orchestras; Mozart and Handel were favourites and in the ninetieth century there were many other composers whose works were known and played in the long winter evenings to audiences drawn not just from the town but from several miles around, despite a hazardous journey in the dark. By the mid-ninetieth century music had become "wet" and unmanly at a time when men were expected to be masculine, moustachioed and bearded, as fitting for Empire-builders. So, too, with poetry. To be a poet was distinctly unmanly, and even Tennyson was frowned upon despite beating the Imperial drum. Then came Elgar to provide music to suit the mood, and Kipling the poetry.

Literature survived with a new style and a heavier substance. Out went the gaiety and *joie de vivre* of Fielding and Sterne or the simple good humour of Goldsmith, Swift and Defoe; in came ornate verbosity, a *genre* more pictorial, with minute descriptions of clothes worn and meals eaten, of which Dickens and Surtees, and sometimes Scott were masters. Like the architecture and the furniture, it replaced plain simplicity with ornate solidity. All three, one felt, were intended for future generations as much as the present, like the Empire itself. Even Thackery and Trollope in their lesser novels tried the patience of readers with whole pages of trivia. A clutch of women writers – Eliot, Gaskell and the Brontes were in a class of their own, but most of the other women writers supplied a demand for sentiment and virtuous values. Many a moral tale was told of how the dispossessed in this life would in the hereafter enjoy much happiness. It did the servants good to read such books, so they said.

Of the other arts, perhaps painting attained the most popularity. The new wealth in new houses had walls to adorn, and what better than an original work of art. The painters no longer scratched a livelihood by travelling from one country house to another to paint a patriarch for future generations to admire; instead artists had their studios in Chelsea or journeyed to romantic corners of the Continent to represent another landscape; and the *noveaux riches* made them a gentlemanly profession. The Royal Academy's summer exhibition drew "all London"; and the great art critic, John Ruskin, was for years a favourite lion of every fashionable hostess. It was Ruskin who said, "Fine art is that in which the hand, the head and the heart of man go together," and he showed how much the art of his time lacked heart. Instead it was respectable, conformist and honest with reality.

The changes may not seem entirely due to the Empire, but also to the Industrial Revolution that brought into being new industries, new towns, new immigrants, as well as a new middle class. But economic historians agree that the Empire and the Industrial Revolution were interacting, each feeding on the other to sustain a parallel growth. Together they gave the English the public schools. Almost a hundred of them were either newly founded or evolved, as noted already, from the old grammar schools. Only a few, like Eton and Winchester, had an ancient lineage. The parents who served the Empire left their children behind to be spared the tropical diseases and to be schooled with their peers, while the new money of the millocrats created a demand for schools to make their offspring into gentlemen. Hence there came into being Harrow, Marlborough, Repton, Rugby, Radley, Bradfield, Cheltenham and a host more, to become a major influence upon the English character. Many young aristocrats still had private tutors, like their fathers and grandfathers, but from now on both Houses of Parliament consisted overwhelmingly of the old boys of these schools; so did the clergy of the Church of England, the judiciary, the university dons, the civil service, the diplomatic and colonial services, and the officers of the Army and Navy, and about half the leading figures in the City and a substantial proportion of professional authors and artists. As the schools were as one in how their pupils should be educated, disciplined and moulded to conform, there can be no mistaking the power they exercised in England's imperial interlude.

A new boy learnt within hours of his arrival that there was a long list of "do's" and "don'ts". They formed a pattern of behaviour which clashed with the instinct to "do one's own thing". The new boy had to conform – nonconformity was as heinous as in religion. Reluctance to conform brought various sanctions; ostracism or bullying by his fellows and a flogging by prefects or masters were the obvious ones. The rules, some written but many devised by the boys themselves, might vary from school to school but never very much. How the cap was worn, how senior boys were addressed, how one cheered the school team. Those made up by the boys themselves were sometimes the most important, for disobedience to them wrought cruel punishment by one's peers. School rules, however, might be broken and lead to a flogging by a master or a prefect, softened by the admiration of those same peers.

Three features in the new public schools combined to change English attitudes – the prefectorial system, team games and the widening of the curriculum to include modern history, geography and English literature. A sense of hierarchy came naturally: new boys were in awe of prefects, prefects deferred to masters and masters to the head. Authority took on a new meaning: boys learnt to sublimate their instinct to be individualistic, and to show respect to those above, and once they themselves attained authority as prefects or team captains, they learnt how to exercise that same authority. To question or challenge those above, as their fathers might have done, was not behaviour acceptable in a rigidly hierarchical society. The boys learnt how to play for the team; keeping the ball to himself in football or rugby in the hope of scoring when a fellow-player was better placed to do so was not something that a boy did twice. The honour of the team was at stake, the honour of the house and the school itself mattered enormously, for all boys shared the honour and when another boy let down the team, house or school, his fellows felt the shame. The English, their individualism ingrained, had to come to terms with a wider view of loyalty. Loyalty to the school and all its segments was extended to one's contemporaries. To sneak was the ultimate crime, and one also learnt to be punished by the beaks with a flogging rather than utter a truth that might bring the same upon another. The reward made it worthwhile; one was judged a man, and all through life it would be remembered by friends made for a lifetime. The imperative of loyalty was not left behind as boys went out of the school gates on their last day. In ships and regiments, in which many of them went to serve, an inflexible code existed as rigorous as at school. In the past, even in Nelson's day, the Navy had its share of buccaneers, and in the Army the officers had little regard for their foreign mercenaries who had formed a large part of the regiments, while their own fellow-countrymen in the ranks were just "the scum of the earth" as Wellington had put it. In those days the officers had scant respect for their superiors and thought nothing of quitting the regiment if called to go abroad or to war. The public school ethic changed all that.

The loyalty reciprocated between the officers and the men was founded upon a simple principle: anything wrong should never be known to the outside world, certainly not another ship or regiment. Regulations of a trivial kind might be broken – so long as honour was saved – but an order disobeyed merited unquestioned punishment. Officers were expected never to let down their men nor the men their officers. My father, who served in the Life Guards, lived in Berkshire but travelled daily to London in alternate years when the regiment was at Knightsbridge, wearing the uniform of a daily commuter – a dark suit and a bowler hat. On one occasion that he had to change into the full uniform and inspect the troops, he duly put on the Wellington boots, red tunic encased in a breastplate, and then instead of the plumed helmet, he replaced his bowler hat. Thus attired he went out to where his groom was waiting for him to mount his charger, but not even out of the corner of his mouth did the groom hiss a word that anything was amiss. As he passed the assembled ranks of the regiment not one of them allowed a flicker of a smile or smirk. And the outside world was never told.

There was loyalty, too, in the commercial world. Boys leaving school joined a firm and commonly stayed a lifetime; and in the smaller business especially the loyalty was repaid in a host of ways as even Dickens would acknowledge. In villages or the streets of towns, when families suffered adversity, others would rally round in ways not found today. Loyalty was a word in regular use in old copies of local newspapers; and gold watches to the long-serving multiplied.

The introduction of team games and putting them on a pedestal of importance higher (at least in the eyes of the boys) than academic achievement went a long way towards instilling the value of loyalty as an integral part of an hierarchical system. The latter, though, was at risk if those above failed to gain the respect of those below; and sheer rank was not enough. The new team games gave the schoolboy the chance to learn how to bring out the best in others, and leadership was also learnt by prefects, monitors, house and school captains. As the public schools raised their standards in the face of competition the prefectorial system changed; the flogging in the better school gave way to other means of getting disorderly pupils into line – by the kind of leadership that could work in later life.

Any human, even small boys, living together in close proximity, cheek by jowl, sleeping in the same dormitory, each bed no more than a foot or two away from the next, eating awful meals elbow to elbow, having to look up at the same master in the same classroom together, playing the same games and doing all this week after week without respite, will be trained to conform. Two crimes became heinous. To steal from another or to tell lies was to proclaim to your fellows you could not be trusted in a tightly-knit society. To dissemble, prevaricate or sink to a half truth was much the same, and to be treated likewise. There is enough evidence to show that before Victoria's reign the English had not always aspired to that standard of integrity, but whatever criticism may be levelled at the public school system, there can be no doubt that it instilled a code of truthfulness that permeated through society. This is not to say that the English were congenital liars until they went to Eton: the English always placed importance upon truth, for they gained a reputation for plain speech on the Continent centuries ago but total truth – the kind a schoolboy can trust in time of trouble – is rather different. In building the Empire, countless treaties and agreements were entered into with native peoples honourably made and their terms honourably kept, and the one or two exceptions were not made by the alumni of the Victorian public school.

By the mid-nineteenth century a distinct change was apparent in the Empire. Although India was not typical of the British possessions, the English who went off to lead most of their lives there – and it was the English who predominated in all the forms of public service there – did indeed go with a high degree of altruism. Missionaries in their thousands made the journey. They were warned beforehand that once there they would have to stay until their mission was over, that they would be exposed to all sorts of diseases for which no remedy might be at hand, that the death rate was high and that they would live in primitive and often squalid conditions with none of the comforts of home life – and for no reward save one. What most of them went through has never been chronicled because only they themselves could tell the story, and only a few morsels were recorded either by or about them. Millions of Indians, though, were inspired to embrace Christianity, and despite becoming a despised minority they are still millions in number. There were also doctors and nurses; they, too, went in their thousands and although they earned a livelihood more than the missionaries, they forewent a more lucrative career at home. Not to be over-looked were the surveyors and engineers who went to build the roads, railways and canals, and many of them died in the task many miles from any doctor to treat them, while others never overcame the effects of malaria for the rest of their lives. Before the Raj, the agencies of government and justice had been corrupt, indeed rotten to the core. The Indian Civil Service and the English judiciary transformed the way British India was administered. If the expatriate judges may have included some who might have had less successful careers at home, that certainly could not be said of the Indian Civil Service. Only men of high calibre, both intellectually and in character, were selected, and it is beyond doubt that they brought the highest standards to the administration. Bribery became unthinkable. The ICS exhibited the best of an English education.

The Blues ruling the blacks, they said about Africa. In the colonies of the dark continent there may have been a somewhat different colonial servant – more likely with a varsity Blue than a First. Perhaps an even less congenial climate than India's demanded a tougher man, but the same standards of integrity prevailed. There, as in the rest of the Empire, the darker side of English individualism was suppressed by the new ethos of the public schools. Individualism was not the only thread of Englishness that became a casualty in the imperial interlude: toleration also suffered. This is scarcely surprising for the two prosper in similar conditions. Uniformity of dress, speech and manners is the outward manifestation of an attitude of mind shared by a class of society, and sometimes as in a region or a walk of life, it will cross the social divisions. Until the mid-nine-teenth century, as social historians have shown, these differences remained most pronounced. The coming of railways and one or two national newspapers enabled more of the English to learn how others behaved; the growth of villages into cities, some as large as Birmingham, attracting tens of thousands from distant parts to form new communities, was another factor. Yet the majority remained in the area where their parents and grand-parents had lived; and only those who could afford the fare – a small minority – travelled far on the new railways. Nonetheless the English were entering a national mindframe, acquiring a uniformity hitherto unknown. They now spoke of themselves as British, as did the Scots and Welsh and even many in Ireland, and not just the Anglo-Irish. The Acts of Union had a part in this new consciousness, but for neither the Scots nor the Irish did a change of the constitution have much practical effect.

Above all, what made them feel British was the Empire. As it stretched outwards, encompassing almost every year yet another segment of the globe, so the pride of being British grew in proportion. Such hubris is intoxicating. The toxicity begets insolence, which never goes hand-in-hand with toleration. That brings a new attitude towards anything or anyone that has the misfortune not to be British. For a nation of twenty-five millions to rule the lives of hundreds of millions became proof enough that there was something special in being British, and no doubt God had ordained it. Greatness came upon the four nations now merging into one. Following naturally came a conscious need to behave as one, even in the minor manifestations of the new mindframe, like speech, dress and manners. Toleration towards those who failed to conform was no longer, for the time being at least, the creed of the English.

But interlude it was. With the Empire gone, we see a return to individualism and toleration. The evidence is all around us. The arts deemed "wet" and unmanly, like poetry, music, opera and ballet, are back in favour. The Anglo-Saxons, let us remember, had composed poetry long before they turned to prose. Individualism has returned to sport as footballers and cricketers display a vanity, once despised, and show that not only opera has its prima donnas. The arrogance of power, the disdain for lesser races and even pride of nationhood has almost vanished. Emotions are no longer bottled up, as the death of Princess Diana demonstrated. Of their fellow countrymen's behaviour, the English have regained the tolerance they showed in Hogarth's time. It shows too in modern dress and manners, no longer ostentatious or even elegant. Morality is relative now, just as it was in Regency times. And the *mores* and rigours of the public school have gone with the Empire too.

Those indices showed how the nation's mood changed with the growth of the Empire. Now they have changed again, becoming similar to what they used to be. Even distinguished novelists, either by their own volition or prompted by their publishers, "put in a bit of sex", just as Smollet and his contemporaries thought they should. Of the 100,000 books published each year at the turn of the century, probably not one of them has been in a style that emulated the Victorians. As for art, architecture and music, conformity has gone with the wind. In Hamlet, we are told "the apparel oft proclaims the man," and anyone travelling among the commuters in London's rush hour will not see the uniform that once proclaimed the businessman and marked him out as "the typical Englishman"; in its place there are a hundred different apparels for every hundred in the throng. Motley, even psychedelic they may be, but these apparels seem to proclaim to us that the English are individualistic once again.

Chapter 8

The European Interlude

When Dean Acheson said, "England has lost an Empire and has yet to find a role," his words cut deeply into many politicians, diplomats and columnists. Coming from a distinguished Secretary of State, reputed to be both an anglophile and a perceptive observer of world affairs, they were painfully poignant. They were said at a time when Parliament was completing a long programme of legislation giving independence to some sixty colonies and protectorates. The British Empire, having become the British Commonwealth, was now to be called merely "The Commonwealth". No longer were retired generals or superannuated politicians to be sent off in their gubernatorial attire, cocked hats included, to salute the lowering of the Union Jack at the going down of the sun: their rule, usually competent and always incorruptible, was to give way to government by the governed. For those who had come to relish the self-esteem and self-importance that are bestowed upon politicians at the heart of a great empire, it was painful to be told that as emperors their clothes were gone. The US State Department, never a friend of the British Empire, had done its utmost to take away the clothes, and now it was hinting that the Atlantic alliance would be strengthened if Britain were to join the European Community. Although it was never said explicitly, the motive was plain. The US wanted Britain as the Trojan horse, an Anglo-Saxon ally that would ensure the Continentals acquired a friendlier stance towards American policy. A Britain in Europe would also stiffen the backbone of the other member-states against the Communist threat both inside the Community and on its eastern frontier. Whenever earnest discussions took place among politicians – and they frequently did – about whether it was desirable to enter the EEC, these points would be made, and again and again the words of Dean Acheson would resonate. Their truth played a major part in steering Britain into the EEC.

That Uncle Sam took active steps to ensure Britain was "in Europe" is now an irrefutable fact. After I became joint chairman of the Get Britain Out Council two Americans came to see me in 1975 with a large bundle of papers. They were, so they claimed, CIA agents who deplored their country's methods in interfering in the affairs of a good ally. What they had brought were copies of documents which showed that a dedicated federalist, Cord Meyer, jnr. was to become head of the CIA station in London for the duration of the Referendum " to do what it takes" to secure a "Yes" vote in favour of Britain remaining in the EEC. The papers showed that the CIA had already given the European Movement considerable sums of money, but now multinational corporations which had been assisted by the CIA were to be persuaded to fund the "Yes" campaign through indirect channels.

I hoped that at least one newspaper would agree to take up the story, but they were all strongly in favour of the EEC, and each one refused. Eventually, in the last few days of the campaign, *Time Out* agreed to publish the story. But it was then a mere fledgling with a small circulation, so only a few hundred Londoners would have read it.

Other people treated my account of the interview with disbelief, and I gave up speaking of the episode. However, the original documents are now filed in Georgetown University. Dr Richard J. Aldrich, an academic of Nottingham University, has examined them and written a research paper about the CIA in Britain based upon the originals,[1] as well as a book.[2]

[1] *OSS, CIA and European Unity* in *Diplomacy and Statecraft*, vol. 8 no 1, March 1997.

[2] Richard J. Aldrich, *The Hidden Hand*; John Murray, 2001.

When in the 1960s a steady flow of parliamentarians travelled to Brussels – almost all of them for the first time in their lives – they received a sympathetic welcome. The first time I went, in 1966, I was invited to a series of lavish meals of a kind not then found in London, and at one of them I remember a kindly Eurocrat putting the case in simple terms. When we had eaten our four or five courses of rich fare and were sipping some excellent brandy, he alluded to the British Empire. "Apart from little Luxembourg," he explained, "the other five of us have all had empires. We got rid of them. They were millstones around our necks. We are richer now and if we unite together we will be richer still because Europe will have the strength to decide the terms upon which we continue to trade with them." His meaning was clear enough: we would all be richer at the expense of our erstwhile colonies. Indeed, that is what has happened. The European Community was never intended to be a free-trade area, but a customs union, as prescribed by the Treaty of Rome. That made it essentially protectionist, inward-looking and economically self-centred. From the time of that conversation I moved rather rapidly towards being an opponent of the whole ethos of the EEC.

To this day the ethos is imperial: the Lomé Convention made supplicants of the erstwhile colonies of western Europe. The ethos is about power, as any talk must be when it is of one group of nations exercising dominion over another. Ought not such talk to be out of date in tomorrow's world?

One thing is clear. That kind of misuse of power has nothing to do with true patriotism. We can be all in favour of England being on the world stage. This book fails in its purpose unless it can show that England should be there, and prominently so. But that is not chauvinism or even nationalism: it is patriotism. A patriot's love for his own country does not require hatred or ill feeling towards any other country, any more than a Londoner's love for his city makes it necessary for him to think ill of Paris or Rome. Love of your country surely implies that there is something about its character so desirable that you wish it to be protected and cherished and are happy to see others emulate it.

There are two ways in which the exportable part of a country's character – its culture – can be emulated by others. One is by the exercise of power, and the other is by mere influence, divorced from power – often spoken of as moral influence. England is uniquely and potentially qualified to have as much influence and probably more than any other country in the world, the United States included. Because such influence is nothing to do with power, whether imperial, industrial or military, size is of little moment. What matters is whether a country has ideas that another believes are worth importing. The smallest country can have this kind of influence as much as any mega-state.

The truth of this came home to me at a conference of parliamentarians in Jamaica that I attended along with delegates from many countries on the other side of the Atlantic. Whenever one of the Canadian representatives rose to speak there was a hush, eyes turned on the speaker and he was heard with rapt attention as none of the others were. Canada exercised no power; neither her armies, diplomats nor business chiefs sought to dominate others, but Canada herself was known to have opened her doors to refugees and given generous help to poorer nations without seeking any advantage in return. She was to all those parliamentarians like a beacon, casting beams of decency, integrity and goodwill to all within her range. On another occasion I was in West Africa, and taken for an American. "No, I'm English," I said rather diffidently, thinking my acquaintance might have bad memories of colonial times. "Oh, that's fine," he replied. "We used to hate the English, but we like them now. Today we hate the Americans for the way they interfere with us."

To bend others to your will by powers of coercion is an obvious way to stir the embers of resentment, and the more it is done the sooner the flames of hostility will blaze. When the European Union imposes trade agreements upon a powerless people it echoes the way in which US transnational corporations have succeeded in acquiring considerable power over the economies of countries in South America. So long as they can buy what they want and sell it elsewhere all may be well. But when they run into difficulties and even their economic power is not enough, the corporations can call upon Washington to exert diplomatic pressure and sometimes military force, and this very possibility creates resentment. More than once an ugly reaction has led to a Communist regime.

The European Community, and in particular the common agricultural policy, has had a dire effect upon the economic well-being of many countries around the world. The evidence of the distress it has caused is overwhelming and fully documented elsewhere. Over the years a long succession of ministers – presidents and prime ministers included – have beaten a path to Brussels to plead on behalf of their countries, most of them former colonies of the European powers. They have been thrown some crumbs in the form of the Lomé Convention and investments of capital which have usually unbalanced their agrarian economies or given the shareholders in Europe a greater gain than the recipients. Having myself visited several countries to see at first hand how their peasant economies have been affected by the common agricultural policy, I believe none with that experience could be left in any doubt about the resentment it has caused; and in some cases, notably in Senegal and Mauritania, desperate poverty and death by starvation.

By erecting trade barriers in agricultural commodities, the mandarins of Brussels have been able to play power politics, and as the Maastricht and Amsterdam treaties transferred to them still further functions of government, their role on the world stage is to be even greater. Any net gain to Britain must be set against the submergence of British interests once she becomes a member-state of the European Union and is left with as much power of self-government as Texas or Virginia.

Lord Palmerston is criticised for having declared "nations do not have friends, they have only interests," but nobody can doubt that Britain's interests are frequently at variance with those of her European partners. Indeed, to call them partners is philological abuse. They are competitors in a single market, and partners and competitors are contradictory terms. A partnership of competitors is a nonsense. So the people of Britain have to make up their minds: they can surrender substantial areas of self-government in return for a share of the hegemonic power of the European Union, but in so doing they will forfeit any hope of moral influence in the world. If the goal of a British government is to recover greatness in the world by forging a partnership with Continental powers, the notion has so many flaws that it is doomed not just to disappointment but to disaster. Ever since Britain joined the EEC in 1973 one attempt after another has been made to Europeanise the British people. Napoleon's metrication was introduced; despite the force of the criminal law, resistance continues, and in some cases successfully – pints of beer and milk can still be lawfully bought and sold and the signposts still speak of miles. But a shopkeeper who obliges an elderly pensioner by allowing her to buy potatoes priced in pounds and ounces, at her request when she is bemused by kilograms, is now committing a criminal offence. Houses built before the 1980s must have their wooden portions replaced with planks and sections that do not fit. That a willing buyer and a willing seller cannot make their transactions in weights and measures of their own free choice without the risk of standing in the dock seems a poor commentary upon a Briton's freedom. The laws about our weights and measures were introduced long ago as means of protecting the public from being cheated. Now they are instruments of coercion.

No one can say with certainty what proportion of our law is now prescribed by Brussels. Since 1973 tens of thousands of statutory regulations have come into our lives, every one of them telling people what they can or cannot do or have. Much of our primary law – the Acts passed by Parliament itself – has its origins in directives from the European Union. The Hansard Society has tried to assess how far the Brussels influence has gone. It concluded that probably forty per cent of all our laws passed since 1973 are due to our membership of the European Union.

If we cannot calculate precisely how much our behaviour has had to change at the behest of Europeanisation, at least there are symbols that are certain. We have a new flag to salute, a new anthem to stir our hearts and a new passport; and the Maastricht Treaty has made everyone in Britain willy-nilly a citizen of the European Union. Would it be too fanciful to suggest that these four symbols of nationhood are intended to condition the British people to feeling European? And have they succeeded or merely aroused suspicion of what is yet to come?

The evidence of our reaction is already apparent. In the parts of the European Union where Brussels has authorised money to be spent more generously than elsewhere, we do not expect to hear ingratitude, hence the murmurings of approval in Scotland and Wales where the EU flag is fluttering over the latest construction funded by "Europe". To make a generalised assessment of English opinion is unwise, for views are heard across the whole spectrum from obsessional faith to rank hostility, and in between there may be a majority whose sullen resignation must be a disappointment to the idealists who dreamed of unity.

The passive sullenness of Albion could yet be inflamed by the example of what is beginning among the more volatile of Europeans. What we are seeing in Europe as in other continents is not the rebirth of nationalism but tribalism. As the first chapter sought to show, this resurgence of a sense of community is part of a paradox: the more the world integrates economically, the more its peoples will strive to cohere in their own social and cultural unities. To be one of those unities, in the opinion of this book, is England's future.

Whether the destination is a federal union or a massive megastate eventually comparable in size with China, there are cogent reasons why the European Union can have no prospect of permanence. The marvels of the electronic age, as the next chapter shows, will frustrate the dreamers of an "ever closer union"; and that apart, the dream overlooks the centrifugal forces in every fusion of unequal parts.

A society of men and women must cohere or fall apart; and the larger it grows in size the more difficult it must be to retain its coherence. Homogeneity is the key to social coherence; and the homogeneity that matters most of all is linguistic. A common language cannot but help lead to a common culture. Not just in Europe but around the world, many attempts have been made to force together nations of different languages. Of the vast number, few have survived more than a century, and mostly they have ruptured within a generation, often in an orgy of violence. The one outstanding exception is Switzerland. That her Germans, Italians and French have managed to live in peace together for half a millennium when beyond the frontier they have been regularly at each other's throats verges upon the miraculous. The reason, though, is simple. Switzerland is divided into twenty-two cantons, each one linguistically homogenous, and no one canton is larger than another. Each being the same in size and strength, none can dominate or threaten a neighbour. Moreover, despite the cantons being only the size of English counties, they are autonomous in almost every activity of government except defence and foreign policy, so there is seldom any cause for conflict between them. In discussing whether Switzerland should join the European Community, the *Wall Street Journal* said it might be more advisable for the Community to join Switzerland. It meant, of course, that if the Community were to adopt a Swiss-style constitution, it might avoid the kind of conflict between the member-states which does so much to blight the hope of unity, as well as softening the fear of the smaller member-states of domination by the Franco-German axis.

As it is, Germany is beyond question the largest of the Community's members, and her size and strength make her the most powerful. Power gained is power to be used and human nature permits few exceptions to the rule. A benign government might well preside over Germany, with her chancellor and ministers reluctant to wield the big stick upon the other member-states; but even if her politicians were of such a kindly disposition, the German people would not for long allow them to be so lily-livered. In a democracy a people denied what they could have, is also an electorate with a power to dismiss.

A federal union can insert into its constitution checks and balances to prevent a larger state dominating a smaller one, as the United States has done. Still more important is cultural cohesion, and whatever their state, there is one America with one culture. Both those advantages are denied the European Union.

Germany is a successful federal union where everyone speaks the same language; the Bavarian feels as much a German as the Prussian, and despite their having, at least to the outsider, a temperament distinctly at variance, they are both indisputably German. Germany is spared the tension that remains a running sore in a federal union which lacks cultural unity, and that ultimately leads to it falling apart. Sometimes the divorce comes amicably as in the case of the Czech Republic and Slovakia, but usually the separation takes an uglier form. No war excretes more venom than a war of secession.

A multilingual continent has given us a multicultural Europe; and multiculturalism in the wider sense, some of us would argue, is her true wealth and glory. How boring it would be to travel around Europe and find everything becoming homogenised. A Marks and Spencer in every market place, the same television programme as at home, the same sort of dishes on every menu, and everywhere no necessity to struggle with another language – why bother to cross the Channel? Such differences that stimulate or irritate the traveller are of no great moment, and we must admit that some are tending to disappear as the peoples of Europe get to know one another better. Of infinitely greater importance are the values and beliefs that can only be truly understood and fully shared among people with a common language, having absorbed what they mean from the books, screen, stage and debate in that language. Put more explicitly, do the English wish to exchange their rule of law with the police methods of France, their religious toleration with that of Spain, their courts of law and sense of justice with those of

Greece or their view of bureaucrats with the Germans? The attempt to create a multicultural megastate of Europe will surely destroy the Continent's multiculturalism in the wider sense if it ever achieves its end; but more likely it will set in train the tensions that end inexorably with its disintegration. History's lesson is that there is no third path for that kind of a state to travel, unless the Swiss model is followed with a nicely balanced rearrangement of parts equal in size and strength. And that is something the European Union will never be.

The size of the European Union raises another difficulty. As I pointed out in *The Breakdown of Europe*, it is at once too small and too big. Europe, properly speaking, is a continent stretching from the Atlantic to the Urals. To deny that Russia and the Ukraine are parts of Europe is not only geographically absurd, but racially and culturally too. Many millions of the citizens of the European Union are genetically indistinguishable from Russians. Tchaikovsky's works are heard as often in London as in St Petersburg; Chekov's dramas in Stockholm as frequently as in Moscow; and Tolstoy's novels are probably read rather more outside the country where they were written than within, Those three, let us admit, belong to all Europe, no less than Beethoven, Shakespeare and Voltaire. Still more important is a fact of history. Europe has been torn apart for centuries and when the Iron Curtain collapsed and the Communists were overthrown, the people had the first opportunity for a thousand years to bring down peacefully the barriers which have stirred so many fears and hatreds – and thus end the curse upon the Continent.

The Treaty of Rome decrees that the Community shall be "an ever closer union" and every day Commission officials go to work to plan the achievement of that aim. The more they succeed in welding together the member-states already in the Union, the more difficult it becomes for newcomers to join. A single currency in a monetary union with uniform interest rates applied across the whole Continent is not believed to be practical, not even by the most zealous of the europhiles, yet nothing could be more calculated to divide Europe than the emergence of two large economic *blocs* – the "ins" and "outs" – with all the potential for conflict between them.

The European Union is too small for another reason. If the purpose of getting nations to act together is to overcome problems they share but cannot effectively cope with on their own, today's Europe cries out for transnational co-operation on a range of environmental issues. Acid rain is destroying vast areas of the forest, particularly in central Europe and Scandinavia. No one country can act successfully to save the trees. Accusations and counter-accusations fly across the frontiers, but no one is certain of the scale of the problem nor who or what is responsible; the only certainty is that unless the countries of Europe reach a common policy and carry out an agreed programme of action the forests are heading for devastation.

Then there is the pollution of both the North Sea and the Mediterranean. Again the European Union is too small to act. Some sixteen countries allow toxic filth into their rivers that flow into the North Sea. The cumulative effect of many years of this pollution is destroying the ecology of northern Europe's most important resource. The common fisheries policy, which requires the former national waters of the member states to belong to the Community and affords equal access to every nation in the Community, has been a prescription for overfishing. The European Union has the power to rectify the overfishing and in particular to end the industrial fishing methods of the Spanish fleets, but seems to lack the will to do so. But the European Union has a valid excuse in not dealing with either the pollution or the over-fishing: only eight out of the sixteen guilty countries are within its jurisdiction. Much the same can be said about the Mediterranean where only four of about ten of the guilty countries are in the European Union.

Even if the European Union were to attempt some common policy to save these two seas, considerable sums of money would have to be spent to achieve success. We can imagine the reaction in Athens, Rome or Madrid if their taxpayers were required to pay more of their money to Brussels to be spent on clearing up the filth caused by northern Europeans. Not even the more phlegmatic British taxpayer is over-eager to do the same for the Mediterranean once the media have told him how the sewers of Athens are emptied.

So long as western Europe remains as densely peopled as she is and enjoys a high standard of living, addicted to growing mass consumerism, her environment will be under attack. Carbon emissions are now reputedly in decline, but are rising rapidly in eastern Europe; tourism, in which hundreds of thousands go to the Alps in winter and summer, is having a dramatic effect upon soil erosion; and to goad farmers with subsidies to increase production is to invite the use of ever more potent pesticides, antibiotics and hormones. In an ideal world these concerns of the present age would be regulated by some authority transcending the globe, but Europe is not yet in utopia, and until she is, the task of saving her continent must rest in her hands. Europe, though, consists of over forty states and the European Union only embraces fifteen. Not unless it brings within its fold the continent as a whole can it undertake the one role that is truly and literally vital. It could also be said that the European Union is hardly entitled to call itself "Europe" when it presides over less than half of what it arrogates to itself.

Paradoxically, the European Union is also too big. We have heard much of its democratic deficit, and how important it is for this to be cured by the European Parliament being given the powers of a proper parliament, especially in matters of legislation and fiscal policy. Theoretically at least, the argument is a powerful one with a particular resonance for the people of England, who have over the centuries spent rather more of their lives in the struggle for democracy than the Europeans. As this book has already pointed out, governments can do absolutely nothing for the benefit of the people they govern unless they first of all take away their freedom (by legislation) or their money (by taxation). Who, then, should decide whether the benefit outweighs the loss? Shipwrecked sailors on their desert island can decide the question among themselves; the Swiss do so when their cantons have a referendum even on minor issues; and no doubt there are communities in many other parts of the world that practise such perfect democracy. Elsewhere representative assemblies must be elected to make the decisions; and as the modern state gathers to itself ever more functions, requiring ever more time of the representatives, so more calls are made upon the political class to rectify the democratic deficit. In the European Union this cannot be the answer for either the British or the Scandinavians, or indeed any nation that has experienced true democracy for any length of time. Merely to elect representatives to decide what laws are to be obeyed or taxes levied is no more than a single step towards the democratic process. A system of proportional representation with a party list of candidates that gives preference to those the party hierarchy chooses severs the link between an individual representative and individual elector. I once asked the late Sir James Goldsmith how large was the constituency he represented in the European Parliament. "All France," was his reply. Unless the law-maker is directly accountable to those who are required to obey the laws made on their behalf the democratic process becomes a sham and there will be little respect for the laws passed. How can one individual be accountable to fifty million other individuals?

Crucial to the principle of accountability is the ratio of legislators to the electorate. Parish councils are inherently more democratic than county councils, and county councils more democratic than the House of Commons. In Brussels or Strasbourg the crucial element of democracy disappears altogether. As a Member of Parliament I have sixty-five thousand constituents and it is just not possible to be democratically accountable to so many. I can answer scores of letters every week, I can issue press releases about what I am doing, and on Saturdays I can go walkabout in the market place, but no matter how hard I try, in the course of the year I can only meet a few hundred constituents – not one per cent of the electorate. Yet politics is about hopes and fears, aspirations and anxieties, and how they can be satisfied or allayed. These are emotions peculiar to each of us and they are not readily volunteered to a stranger. After a few years a Member of Parliament may acquire an instinctive feel for those emotions but only in general terms.

For members of the European Parliament, even with a system of direct elections, the ratio is 1:500,000. With the system of proportional representation adopted for that parliament, the ratio breaks down and constituencies consist of millions. Links of communication so indispensable to the principle of accountability, are ripped out. The advent of television takes their place, so it is claimed, but does it? It would be difficult to devise a more comfortable way of communicating with a mass audience, but it is essentially a one-way dialogue. Worse than that, it produces a feeling of powerlessness in the elector, and that by definition is the denial of democracy. It also gives to the politician a degree of additional power – bad for his ego, and a decisive step towards authoritarianism.

Television having intruded upon our politics it is not going to go away, yet for the English, who are reputed to head the world's league table for addiction to the small screen, it has a relevance in the context of European governance. When I first stood for Parliament in 1950 in a mining and steel town, the safe Labour seat of Rotherham, I spoke at two public meetings every night of the campaign; in the morning and at the lunch hour. I spoke outside the mills and plants; most afternoons there were more meetings for particular groups like pensioners, women, schools and business people. I canvassed not a single house, and all I did for some two and a half weeks was to carry on an active dialogue with audiences that in total constituted a large proportion of the electorate. Unlike today, every elector had the opportunity to make the candidate accountable. In the General Election of 1951 I was a candidate in a rural constituency which was marginal. Here the meetings were even more frequent – three or four every evening, for every village expected the opportunity of hearing and questioning the man who might represent them at Westminster. Conservatives came to support, opponents came to heckle and almost always there were many undecideds who came to make up their minds. Any speaker had to be on his toes. Without a doubt it was democracy at work. Anyone in the audience with a tongue in his head was given a taste of power; anyone could get the candidate to commit himself to a future policy or be forced to argue to the contrary. Furthermore, the candidate knew that after he was elected he would have to face an audience at further meetings and tell them convincingly about his record on their behalf. If he failed to convince them he might lose the seat, as many did.

The 1951 General Election was the last in which television played no part, and it was not until after polling day that, on visiting a supporter, I saw a television set for the first time. It was believed to be the only one for miles around. By the time of the next election, in 1955, there were thousands of homes with sets; the effect upon the democratic process had begun. (It was the first general election when counts were televised and my return for Billericay was the first.) From then on, the dialogue of the public meeting went into decline, replaced by the monologues from the screen. Candidates now just canvass; hurriedly glad-handing as they hasten from one doorstep to the next, and by polling day they encounter an insignificant fraction of the people who once could publicly call them to account. Democracy has gone backwards.

Although there can be no return to the 1950s, which was probably the highpoint in Britain's history of democracy, there can be a resolve to fight any further loss of the power the individual once possessed. If the principle of accountability scarcely exists when the ordinary citizen has just one vote among many millions, how much less accountable will the politician be when it is one vote among hundreds of millions? This staggering democratic deficit should be, for the ordinary people of England, a paramount argument against Europe's "ever-closer union".

A political union (and no one doubts that a monetary union must lead to it) enfolding not less than 350 millions of many nations, languages and cultures will be the very negation of democracy. Democracy has been described as the diffusion of power. But a political union which consists of half of Europe will necessitate a massive transfer of legislative and fiscal power to Brussels and Strasbourg; and the individual's right to hold the politician accountable will vanish.

The Treaties of Rome, Maastricht, Amsterdam and Nice are not to be the last of the ratchets over which the peoples of Europe will be pulled towards the "ever closer union". The sense of nationhood has been attacked by the symbols of a new flag, a new anthem and a new passport as well as a new citizenship. There is also the Committee of the Regions, set up by the Maastricht Treaty, and potentially the greatest threat of all to Englishness. The new Regions cross the national frontiers; Northumberland becomes part of Scotland; Kent is joined with Nord Pas-de-Calais, and to its west a new Region is called East Sussex-Haute Normandie-Picardie. The two latter are not fanciful plans by an idle dreamer in Brussels; one of them has been allocated £62 millions of Community funds and the other £53 millions. Among the Regions decided upon is Ulster, which takes from the Republic the counties of Louth and Monaghan, which may excite a few people once it is more widely known. The objective, it is obvious, is to uproot patriotic instincts that go with a sense of country. Only one or two more treaties may complete the process of not just economic and political integration but cultural too. That this is no whimsical threat is proved by the map of the European Union published by the Commission. England is not there. She is obliterated. In her place are named Regions. Of all the countries of the European Union, England alone is threatened in that way.[1]

The English, then, have reason enough to question where the European Union may take them. England's history since the Conquest from Magna Carta onwards has been a long march from the dictatorship of a monarch to a form of constitutional

[1] As a result of many protests, it is believed the map is going to be amended to include England.

government, wholly in keeping with Anglo-Saxon culture and radically different from the Continental tradition.

Do the English therefore disentangle themselves from the European Union? If the answer is affirmative, it does not follow that they turn their backs upon their neighbours on the Continent. Europe needs some institutional structure to enable her peoples to face some of the problems that cross the frontiers. The argument advanced in this chapter suggests a looser association, but one in which all parts of Europe belong as of right. A bureaucracy based in any one capital that decrees what should be done or not done throughout all member-states, especially when decided by majority voting, epitomises the mischief of making decisions "top-down". If any government in any corner of Europe believes it shares with others a problem that can best be overcome by transnational cooperation, then it ought to be able to turn to some European institution to co-ordinate the necessary action. The Council of Europe, the Economic Commission for Europe under the UN and the Council for Security and Co-operation in Europe have each in their way advanced pan-European co-operation, and each could do much more. But the European Union has frequently stood in the way, jealously protecting its ambitions to act for "Europe". Between the European Union and the other three institutions there is a sharp difference in how they function. The former acts supra-governmentally, the others inter-governmentally. The member states of the European Union, by allowing their own legislatures and judiciaries to be subordinated to the supra-governmental counterparts, have forged the essentials of a mega-state. Whether it evolves into a federal union or a unitary state, is yet to be discovered: whichever it is, the consequences for England especially are tragically obvious. If the European Union cannot be persuaded to retreat from its supra-governmental goal, the future for England lies either in abandoning her core values and beliefs, to end her existence by being carved up in Regions and ruled in ways alien to her past, or in negotiating an amicable withdrawal and bringing to a close her European interlude. If

she did that she would still be free to accede to all inter-govern-
mental endeavours of the Continent consistent with her legiti-
mate interests, and that would be an alternative that her
neighbours would be unwise to reject, as to do so would be to
put their own interests at risk. England is of Europe. Both geography and history have locked her in with some forty or more
European countries. What matters for the peace and harmony of
the Continent is that all forty or more should have the means of
living together as good neighbours. It is a true saying that good
fences make good neighbours, and one that applies to nations
too. Unfortunately, the European Union, in its zeal to remove
barriers, is tearing down too many of the good fences with them.

Chapter 9
A Future Greater than the Past

If we can draw a distinction between power and influence, in the way the previous chapter suggested, how may the latter contribute to England's future? Can a country geographically small, overpopulated and industrially no longer the world's leader, be in a position to exercise influence on the international stage? Besides, does it matter whether the English have a role in the world or will it be more congenial for them to live quietly by themselves, like most other nations, unconcerned by what others say or do?

Looking carefully at what is happening around the world, it can become apparent to the English that the answers to the questions posed are not so hard to find. Three great events are happening. They are interconnected and interacting upon each other. Together they will make the world of the twenty-first century very different from what it is today – so different that every nation, indeed every single person, ought to consider the effect these three factors will have upon their own countries, their own lives and those of their children. What is more, these three events are potentially capable of changing life in England more radically than in any other part of the globe.

The first of these events has been widely discussed already, the advent of the global economy, supranationally regulated by the World Trade Organisation. The second, although much discussed, has a significance that few of us have so far comprehended: the electronic revolution. The third is the paradox that the more the world integrates economically the more people in every continent are striving for self-determination. The third is a reaction to the first event and facilitated by the second.

These three events share a language. It is the language England has given to the world. Almost everything said or done to further the global economy has been in English, and the World Trade Organisation thinks, deliberates and drafts its numerous documents in the tongue it knows best. That the accent and spelling is American does not really matter.

English is the one language that can serve technology most effectively, and its use has become imperative in commerce, banking, diplomacy, aviation, international law and, indeed, whenever the East converses with the West. French, once the language of world diplomacy, has been replaced. Men and women were considered uneducated, not just in Europe but in most capitals around the world, unless they could converse in that language. Now English has taken its place, and it is doubtful whether there is a single country where English is not taught in the leading schools. To deprive their pupils of the opportunity to learn English is to set them back in any career of commercial, scientific or diplomatic consequence. That the Americans play a decisive role in making English the means of communication between one nation and another is a fortunate legacy of the imperial interlude, just as Latin was of Rome.

The breaking up of the larger political unions into smaller culturally united states also owes much to the English language. These ruptures may come by violent means, but their origin lies in the communication of an idea. Although what is said and written will be in the tongue of the aggrieved people, their leaders will have acquired the values and beliefs that uphold the dignity and self-worth of an independent and sovereign people, all of which have been expressed more cogently in English than any other tongue.

After the late Charles Clore had become a millionaire many times over he was asked how he had managed to succeed so quickly. "Maximise assets" was his abrupt reply. It is not an analogy to press too far, but for a nation, as for a man or woman, in search of a new role, the advice seems as obvious as it was to Clore. England has given her people a number of assets, but in tomorrow's world where communication between peoples is going to be possible in a way it could never have been in the twentieth century, language – the ability to speak and write so that others can understand and the command of words that can persuade and cajole, as well as converse in friendship – is surely an asset beyond price. The imperial interlude gave it to the English: the European interlude may not take it away, but it will be diminished when a German or Frenchman or any of the others stands upon the world stage to speak for Europe and negotiate on behalf of the European megastate.

If the three interlaced events are to make the world such a different place, where will they or can they take England? Between "will" and "can" there is a serious difference. Remaining in the European Union, and made into one of its dependent regions, the English will be of no more account than the Walloons or Bavarians. Such a future betrays their past; and betrays those millions who, because the English example is no longer available, will be denied the right to live in that state of wider freedom that is as much political, cultural and economic as it is social and personal. For how can the values and beliefs of England be exported around the world to those who would wish to embrace them if England herself is but a province of somewhere else, and the English no longer a sovereign people governing themselves?

The birth of the global economy, achieved in the English language, is but a recent event, a small child with a long way to go until adulthood, with total unfettered free trade between all peoples of the world. That stage, of course, may never be reached; a recession will retard progress and the fear of Asian growth may make the West pull up the drawbridge. One or two facts sum up the danger. A Chinese skilled with a computer may earn one tenth of the income of his counterpart in Britain. Yet it is now technologically feasible for a car or tractor to be physically made in Coventry, but every human engaged in the process to remain in the middle of China. What hope, then, of full employment in the West? If something so intricate as a car or tractor can be manufactured in that way, we can see a prospect of an immense upheaval with consequences as much social and political as commercial and technical. To ponder on this for no more that half a minute is to conjure up a veritable nightmare: ten million British jobs computerised and lost to Asia; investors, led by fund managers in control of pensions, transmitting billions of pounds of capital out of the country; houses unsaleable, taxes no longer capable of being paid, a government bankrupted and...

When that scenario begins, there could be a simple solution. The ideal of universal free trade may be commendable: it is grounded on the tenet that a willing buyer and a willing seller should be free to meet to their mutual advantage, and the fact that one lives in one country and the other somewhere else should not matter. The more the peoples of the world trade together amicably, the less likely are they to exchange nuclear missiles. "When goods do not cross the frontiers the soldiers will," said the Victorians. But these fine words presuppose that the international trade is conducted fairly and perceived to be fair. We have to ask ourselves whether Asian manufacturers whose wage costs – quite apart from other elements – remain one-tenth of what they are in the West will pass the test of fairness. No matter what some moralist may say to the contrary, if several millions lose their jobs as a result of a massive flow of imports we cannot assume they will just shrug their shoulders with indifference at the prospect of remaining out of work for the rest of their lives. A floating exchange rate can rectify a modest imbalance of trade, and of all forms of import control it is unquestionably the speediest to take effect and the least arbitrary or bureaucratic, but something more drastic than that will be needed if the scenario begins to materialise.

What is of major importance for the country in danger is to have a range of policies from which to choose at the time, so that the most effective can be adopted. Country A may want to act differently from Country B. For example, certain textiles are being imported to Britain now which are remarkably cheap and undercut the home produced products. They are also exported to other parts of the European Union. This is fine for countries which do not manufacture textiles for they benefit when the money saved goes to buy something else. But Britain will have another few hundred out of work; and once British production comes to an end, the Asian exporter will have a monopoly and up will go the prices. This has happened with several kinds of goods already. Britain, however, like the other member-states of the Union, has lost the right to take unilateral action. All trade policy matters being vested in the EU Commission, no action is taken while the other countries enjoy the benefits of cheap imports. Besides, the procedure in Brussels is ponderous and cumbersome: frequently it can take months to reach a decision which may end in a compromise less effective than unilateral action. For any state, large or small, to surrender its power to protect itself in distress is foolhardy. It may prove worse than foolhardy as the global economy grows from its present infancy to adulthood.

When the Great Slump struck in the 1930s every industrialised country suffered, but the suffering was not uniform, some going through a period of mass unemployment and desperate hardship far worse than others. Although the period has been well chronicled by economic historians, one significant feature has escaped the notice it deserves. There was a correlation between the size of an industrialised country and the devastation that followed. Big countries suffered more than small ones. The biggest economy suffered most of all, and that was the United States. The slump also lasted longer in big countries; despite Roosevelt's New Deal, the US recovery had begun only falteringly by 1939. On the other hand Sweden, although per capita more industrialised than the US, had got over the worst of the slump within a year or two. The contrast is not difficult to explain. The smaller the scale of a problem, the easier it is to overcome; that general rule applies especially with something as complex as the malfunctioning of a country's economy. In a big state the government will resort to remedies that blanket every corner of economic activity, such as the raising of tariffs or the lowering of interest rates. This may suit some parts of a blighted economy, but not all. Both the United States and Britain had to act in this way. An across-the-board tariff went a long way to resuscitate certain industries, motor car manufacturing for example, but it also raised the price of many articles, which added to the cost of living and reduced people's spending power, thus preventing them from buying other goods or services provided by the domestic market. Jobs gained by one major industry could lead therefore to jobs lost in many minor ones. In a small country with fewer industries affected by imports the government can target the tariffs on where they will help, and they can do so speedily. A small country in the global market place can be likened to a frigate out at sea; it can twist and turn at speed unlike a great ocean tanker, twenty times the size, which needs a mile or more to change its course.

Like the ocean tanker, the European Union may prove too big: come a world slump, it could suffer as much as, perhaps more than, the United States did in the 1930s. Of course, it is big enough to be heard in the World Trade Organisation, but once the groundwork for a global economy is complete, where is the economic advantage of EU membership? The small self-governing country then has the dual advantage: the freedom to trade in the world's market place, while retaining the protection of a floating exchange rate and control over interest rates, both being dependent upon a national currency of its own.

In the global economy it will not be just tariff-free goods that cross the frontiers, but capital, and to an extent far greater than today. This transfer of invested money will have its hazards for developing countries and for any economy signalling stagnation. Anyone responsible for investing other people's money is in a highly competitive business where success is easily measured and failure severely penalised. The responsibility demands several talents, integrity and experience in particular, and in only a few centres has the investor found those qualities, Hong Kong, Tokyo, Singapore, Sydney, Paris, New York, Frankfurt and London. Of these, the last is still pre-eminent, but only just. Both Germany and France, eager to grasp a larger slice of the palatable cake, have tried to devise new rules in the EU to curb the flexible and informal practices of London, but not in Paris or Frankfurt. Again, this is a threat that can be countered by self-government, and it needs to be, for those two traits of the City have done as much as anything to keep England in the prime position. As a City of international investment it contributes mightily to England's wealth. As the business of transferring invested money around the world grows – as it will in a global economy – so will the City's contribution. To take but one example, pension funds are still only for a minority in the West, yet they contain many thousands of billions of pounds and they are expanding rapidly: eventually it is probable that it will be normal for most people in the world to be contributing in some way to these funds. Half a century hence, the management of pension funds could become the largest service industry of all. For London to be at its heart is more than a possibility. The City's square mile is an asset to be maximised, but will it be if control of monetary, fiscal and regulatory policies passes to Brussels and Frankfurt?

But in the global economy is there not a danger that the great transnational corporations will trample upon the small country? The moguls in command of these monsters see the danger in a different light. A self-governing country, whatever its size, has the power to legislate and tax as its government or parliament considers necessary. In a democracy, we hope, it will have the support of its people for the laws passed or the taxes imposed. Whether a democracy or not, it will always be able, through the media, to articulate to the public – and to the world outside if need be – the reasons for what it is doing, in a way that no transnational corporation would have the money or ability to do. A contest between a democratically elected government and the moguls would be an unequal battle. Such contests seldom occur, but what has happened in Britain already is the *sotto voce* threat to close a car manufacturing plant, with a hint that another government has offered to fund it more favourably. Such overtures are made over the table to a minister or civil servant, and if they cannot cope with the threat they are scarcely fit to hold their office. No doubt there are occasions when the moguls succeed with this approach, although the evidence that they do comes from other countries.

On the other hand, there is no doubt that the transnational corporations favour the creation of megastates. How very tiresome it would be for them to trade in the European Union if the fifteen member-states retained their self government with each having different regulations to govern the quality and sale of their products. Nobody could have been more eager to complete the single market than the heads of these corporations. They have met together to confer how it could be done; the chairmen of the main corporations, originally seventeen of them and now over thirty, have found it worth their while to meet and discuss their common objective and to plan the steps towards it. Between them they have collected many millions of pounds to be spent upon promoting the European Union. Much of the money has been donated to organisations like the European Movement which openly admits that it works for a political union and the submergence of all the countries of western Europe into a superstate. A politically and economically inte-grated superstate would suit the moguls' book, for they could then operate as they believed most profitably to themselves. No need then for them to do anything so disagreeable as to threaten the ministers of a small state, for the decision is simply made in the board room and carried out when convenient.

The advantage to the transnational corporation goes rather further than that. Many of these thirty or more have offices in Brussels, close to the Commission's offices. No selling or mar-keting, and certainly no manufacturing is done in any of them. The corporations are large enough to afford such offices for full-time lobbyists, and they find it easy enough to make contact with the officials who draft the regulations or allocate the subsidies and regional funds. Mid-day is the time for a large lunch when lobbyists and officials can be seen at one of the many restaurants that prosper in Brussels. Thus new laws are made and no one is there to speak for the small businesses trying to compete against the major corporations, nor does the consumer have more than a muted voice. These lobbyists are also in a position to arrange non-tariff barriers against imports that might damage their interests, for on several occasions this has been done by the Commission with astonishing speed. Acting in this way an ICI lobbyist once nearly ruined a small importer in my constituency, and it took several years for the firm to recover from the loss.

It would be going too far to claim that all the advantages in a global economy were with the small self-governing countries, but when the arguments are laid out on each side of the scales, every economist seems to have come down on the side of the small against the big. Living and working and above all trying to carry on a business in one big open world may make us a little nervous, and to shelter behind the protection of a giant may sound attractive. But sentiments like those have no place in the heart of the truly enterprising, nor should men and women with skills and energy be fearful. The important fact is that smaller businesses prosper in the domestic market; and in a small country the voice of small business is heard.

This brings us to an intriguing paradox. The telecommunication revolution, having enabled the global economy to be born, is changing the nature of the great international corporations. Deconstruction is taking place; the main boardrooms of these corporations are devolving the decision-making to autonomous divisions. Those that operate in many countries have learnt that fashions can change quickly, and not simultaneously in every country. In some, customers are more discerning than in others. The balance between price and quality will vary from one people to another, and even in the same country it will not be the same throughout. These pressures upon even the largest of the transnational corporations, and their consequent deconstruction, have gone a long way towards removing the threat that once was feared.

But surely these pages have said enough about the economics. Turning the globe around we can find at least twenty countries much smaller than England and every one of them more prosperous *per capita*. Some are no larger than Surrey, Dorset or Durham; several in Europe have a population no bigger than market towns like Banbury, Taunton or Skipton. Is the mother country of the Industrial Revolution afraid of the independence that they enjoy?

We have already noted how multicultural unions are breaking up, how and why it will happen in the United Kingdom, how the number of countries passing the test of being self-governing and eligible to join the United Nations is forecast to go on increasing. These countries are now component parts of larger states, so the disintegration of those unions which we witness today is a process that will accelerate as the electronic age changes the world. It confounds the long-held theory of history that it is mankind's destiny to form ever larger units, from the primitive family of the first *homo sapiens* to the tribe, from the tribe to the nation and, centuries later, to unions of nations, and ultimately to world government. Instead, we are moving towards a world market place, but possibly a thousand governments.

This rise in the UN membership confirms the urge inherent in men and women for independence. Until now the means to achieve it have not been available for those many millions living under any sort of authoritarian rule, unless they resorted to the barricades. By the year 2015 they will resort to the marvel of telecommunications to gain their objective, for that is the date that Bill Gates predicts for the near universal use of the latest telecomputer.

In *The Breakdown of Europe*[1] I set out in detail some ways in which the telecommunications revolution will radically change

[1] Richard Body, *The Breakdown of Europe*; New European Publications, 1998.

social and political life. (Much of it was based on John Naisbitt's seminal book *Global Paradox*.) It will be useful to summarise the argument here and to see how it will bear on the English in particular.

The process starts with the hybridisation of computers, telephones and television. The ways in which they are now being linked together allow the ordinary citizen not just to receive unprecedented amounts of information but also to interact with others and to send out information and opinions of his own through a world-wide network of communication.

From this it follows that global alliances can quickly be formed between people with common aims and interests. Until now that has been a slow and cumbersome business. Direct contact with a hundred people meant a hundred letters or telephone calls and getting them together for a discussion of their aims and strategies could take many hours of effort. In the new electronically linked world one person will be able to launch his ideas to an unlimited number of others, and if they arouse an enthusiastic response a new and powerful movement could start to roll forward immediately. Question and answer, proposal and response, now flash backwards and forwards not in days or weeks as they used to but literally in seconds.

Two points arise from this. First, neither distance nor international frontiers will pose any sort of barrier. The question of whether people communicating in this way live under the same government or a number of different governments will be simply irrelevant. The second, and important, point is that when an alliance is formed on some political question it will create a challenge to the democratic process in its present form. Politicians and civil servants will be bombarded with messages demanding answers, action, information, consultation. When these messages emanate from powerful alliances they will not be able to ignore them. What will it be like in Brussels in 2015 when hundreds of pan-European alliances have been formed? It hardly needs to be pointed out that the larger the political unit, the more danger it is in of being swamped by this process.

Another significant point is that what will develop will not be just a network of telecommunications but a network of networks. As an example, suppose that some important new research is being done in the field of human genetics. Obviously this will be communicated to the network of geneticists working in universities and commercial laboratories. But it will also go out on the networks of scientific journalists, ethical philosophers, Roman Catholic priests and perhaps a number of others. Soon it will be widespread enough for anyone who wishes to take part in the debate to have his or her say via the world-wide interactive web of communication that will then exist.

No doubt much of what is fed into the web will be eccentric and even nonsensical, but it will at least be a melting pot in which old prejudices and preconceptions will be broken down, and every now and then a consensus will form on some new programme of action that will be sensible enough for politicians to have to take it seriously and adapt their policies to it.

In this way ordinary people will become empowered to an extent they have never been in the past. The danger some people foresee is that this power will be concentrated in the hands of a new elite, those who have acquired mastery over the complex techniques of the electronic age, and the rest will form an underclass of computer-illiterates. Almost certainly this is a groundless fear. As computers develop they become more and more user-friendly. A computer of the future will be capable of guiding the most unknowledgeable user, instructing him in easy-to-understand ways on how to make the best use of it. The more sophisticated the computer, the less sophistication it will need to operate it, and already it is no more necessary for a user to understand how computers work than it is for someone watching television to be able to build a television set. We can foresee a time, too, when computers will be available in public libraries, civic offices and official agencies, with qualified staff in attendance to help anyone handicapped by poverty, illiteracy or others problems.

All this will have an incalculable effect on the world of politics. At the extreme, some people foresee politicians becoming obsolete and countries being governed through a sort of permanent electronic plebiscite. According to this scenario, the telecomputer of the future will be able to receive, store and process all the information that is available to the government. The ordinary members of the public will have full access to it and will be able to vote electronically for what they want done. We can be fairly sure that it will never quite come to this, for many decisions can only be taken by people who spend their lives mastering the problems concerned. It is better for the bank rate to be determined by a dozen experts than by the majority vote of fifty million people, most of whom have not given ten minutes' thought to the matter.

Nevertheless there are many political issues where the consensus of ordinary citizens is at least as likely to be a better guide to action as the decision of a cabinet concerned inevitably with preserving power for its own party as much as with the country's welfare. Already politicians spend a lot of time and resources trying to find out, through polls and focus groups, what ordinary people want them to do. (When the resulting decision goes the way you approve it is called democracy. When it goes the other way it is called naked populism.) The new technology will allow politicians to keep in much closer and more immediate touch with public opinion: indeed it will make it impossible for them to avoid it. Even if this does not obviate the need for a professional structure of government consisting of ministers and civil servants, it will certainly have an impact on the functions of a parliament whose power is already much diminished compared with that of the executive.

England being in the forefront of electronic technology will become one of the first countries to embark upon this kind of democracy. Provided that she has regained her homogeneity – and it is important proviso – democracy will be immeasurably strengthened by this new process of government. One hopeful thing is that homogeneity will itself be greatly strengthened by a further effect of the new technology, the freedom it gives people to choose the places and even the countries where they live and work. It will no longer be necessary for them to cluster together in cities with people engaged on the same job as themselves. A man or woman at a computer keyboard can be linked to and work with someone at another keyboard a thousand miles away as easily as with someone in the next room. People will be able to live wherever they find the people, the culture and the climate most agreeable. It may seem paradoxical, but the effect of this will not be to merge different cultures with each other but to make them more distinctive, and England will be a prime illustration of this.

At present there are many people – hundreds of thousands and perhaps even millions – who are tied to England by their occupation but who would rather live in Tuscany or somewhere else more to their taste and outlook. In future many of them will be able to migrate to where they would wish to be. Their departure will make England more English. Then there may be large numbers of people in other parts of the world who have learnt about England and her culture and who think they would prefer to live in such a country. If they too have occupations that can in the future be carried on in England as well as where they are now they will migrate to England – and they will be immigrants for the best of reasons. They too will make England more English. England, which has always been multiracial, may become more so, but she will gain in cultural homogeneity and social cohesion.

And it is social cohesion that is the vital element in overcoming the sense of alienation that so many people now feel. One third of young people now go to a university or some form of higher education; they are given an opportunity for a career and have their share in the country's prosperity. But what of the remaining two thirds? Perhaps a majority will settle down to an equally worthwhile occupation, not so well paid but nonetheless affording a measure of contentment. That may still leave several tens of thousands every year joining the million or more who are unemployed and often unemployable, and who – as an increasing number do – want to contract out of normal living. The latter includes the drop-outs, the drifters, the many thousands who turn to drugs and their *demi-monde*, not temporarily but self-rejected from society in search of an alternative culture. Then there are the many (and there are very many more than there used to be) for whom crime is a way of life. One of the changes that have come over the English in the last two or three decades is the fear of the stranger. Even in the countryside it is rare to find a front door unlocked; shops have costly surveillance monitors, and far too many are fearful to walk down their own street at night. Law and order has become a political issue ranking high in priority for millions of English people.

In the 1930s crime was negligible. In most towns and villages a locked door was considered anti-social, and rather a slight upon neighbours. Judges on assize would spend no more than a day or two as they paid their stately visit to the country town; now these towns will have two or three judges sitting all the year round.

So what has gone wrong? In the 1930s there was poverty and hunger, and the average wage was £2 a week. "Poor but honest" is an old saying, and a true one, for the really poor have only their self-respect, which is lost with a crime committed. Acute poverty, especially when children went hungry, no doubt led to thieving, but today a system of social security rarely allows the acutely poor to slip through the net. We must look for some other explanation for this alienation of which crime is but one manifestation.

Self-respect or self-esteem is not necessarily a view of oneself as an individual. The individual can escape from his own limitations by being part of a nation; and a belief that one's nation is good or great allows one to share that goodness or greatness. When Britain was a great power, every British man or woman could feel themselves great. The history taught in the schools was about battles won and an empire gained, and how well it was ruled. With the geography lesson the atlas was studied and pupils gazed at all the pink. Even in the literature lesson the only books read were by fellow countrymen, as if none other was capable of writing a book worth reading. A few days ago I returned to the history book of my pre-war school days; as I turned over the pages, I was made to realise what achievements had been made by the English, Scots and Welsh. Were anyone to read no other history book, they would be convinced that the British were the only people who mattered. No such book is in the schools today. The history children are taught is almost anti-British and certainly not flattering to the English.

The average schoolchild will sit, so we are told, as many hours before a television set as in the classroom. Has anyone seen a television programme that puts Britain or the British, let alone England and the English, in a favourable light? Self-mockery is an English trait and scarcely a fault, but when it comes to the mass media it may be necessary to ask whether it is not time for a little more balance. Moreover, self-mockery naturally follows from self-confidence for only the self-assured can risk the mocking; but once self-confidence has been destroyed, it is time the self-mocking came to an end. And quite plainly all those who are permanently unemployed, the criminal *demi-monde* or the otherwise alienated, know no self-confidence born of pride of country. When England becomes more English as the electronic age progresses, cultural homogeneity will be regained and with it a clearer consciousness of what it means to be English. The alienated will be as empowered as the rest of us and their self-rejection from society no longer need be made. The social consequences will be as far reaching as the political. A society that feels united and held together by a sense of pride and confidence in England ought to be a less fearful homeland than she is today.

Now let us consider the arts in its widest term. The last half century is the period when there has been such uncertainty about England and Englishness and in that time the arts have not inspired people as they did in previous periods. Architects have given us blocks, high and square and so far from what is natural (for nothing in nature is square) that they are meaningless and ugly. The Prince of Wales raised his voice on behalf of the rest of us and the architectural establishment howled, but it could not deny that too many in its profession had prostituted themselves to appease a type of developer who would be chased away in any town in France or even Italy.

What is true of architecture is true of others arts. How much music has been composed in the last half-century that draws people into concert halls? How many of us actually buy the works of our painters and sculptors out of our own earnings? Perhaps that is not the most satisfactory test, but it was the one in ages past and it bequeathed to us so much of what we value today. The cinema is transatlantic. Only the theatre seems to compare well with what other generations have known. It is at least arguable that this decline stems also from a nation's malaise.

Some Europhiles maintain that our artistic decline will be reversed if we join in a single political block with the other nations of Europe. It is an enticing idea but it is almost certainly the reverse of the truth. Creative cross-fertilisation occurs when a lively native culture comes in contact with exciting new ideas which have been developing independently in another culture. This happened, for example, when English architects were confronted with the radically different work of Renaissance Italy. The fusion of the two disparate traditions produced a new and distinctively English form of architectural classicism that is still one of the glories of our towns and countryside. Unfortunately the situation today is entirely different. Our style of architecture, at any level above the suburban semi, is not indigenous but cosmopolitan. Our own native tradition is diluted and the ideas that come to us from continental Europe are those we are already familiar with. The "shock of the new" stopped being either shocking or new a long time ago.

It is also a fallacy to suppose that art will thrive most in a very large political or social unit. We have only to look at the great creative centres of excellence in the past to see that. The peak of English drama came not in the huge, rich, imperial London of the Victorian age but in the comparatively tiny city of Tudor and Jacobean times. Periclean Athens, the cradle of European thought was by our standards a small provincial town. The great traditions of German music and philosophy flourished before Germany, as a single state, existed at all.

English art over the centuries, like that of every other country in Europe and probably the world, has prospered most when it has expressed its own distinctive values and beliefs yet not been isolated from art elsewhere. There will be no danger of isolation when the telecomputer gets to work, and no question of England pulling up the drawbridge against the world. The twenty-first century can see the English on the world stage; indeed in an electronic age, an open economy encompassing the globe will make it impossible for them to be Little Englanders, even if they had the urge to turn their backs upon their own culture, traditions and history, as well as the temperament of their forebears.

A nation, let us remember, is a collective of men and women living together, within certain frontiers and united by the same core values and beliefs. It may or may not claim greatness by the exercise of power over other nations, unfettered by moral principles. That kind of greatness evokes sullenness, resentment and other reactions which are all malign. Another kind of greatness is one we have experienced in our everyday lives: it belongs to the men and women who have influenced us for the better, and who have earned our respect and admiration. As with individuals so with their collectives. And why not that role for the English?

What matters is that there are some distinctive qualities of Englishness that the English people themselves need to recognise. That done, they will realise that the twenty-first century can offer an opportunity for England to influence the world in ways that today may be difficult fully to comprehend. But the English people must first of all recover their right to govern themselves, then they can determine how to lead their lives according to their own inherited values and beliefs bequeathed to them down the centuries, and without them being compromised as they are now by the need to share their government with others whose culture is different. Only with that right regained, is it possible for all whose domicile is English, whatever their birth, upbringing or racial origin, to have a sense of shared identity and a modest pride in being what they are. But to achieve that some practical steps must also be taken within England herself.

Chapter 10
The Practicalities

As the exit of Scotland, Ulster or Wales will force the demise of the United Kingdom, the English will have no alternative but to come to terms with what will in due course be a fact of history. For an older generation – anyone over, say, fifty at the turn of the century – it will be painful, seemingly unrealistic and perhaps beyond their comprehension. They were born the children of a mighty imperial power at the very heart of Western civilisation which was also a great centre of international trade, made possible by a fusion of factors, each one the consequence of some form of power. To them the very notion that little England could survive in the world all on her own, isolated and deserted by her fellow islanders, may be quite absurd, at best a romantic dream and at worst plainly suicidal.

Yet England even on her own would have the seventh, perhaps the sixth, largest economy in the world. By any reckoning, there are 150 other national economies (and arguably there are over 200) which are smaller. What is encouraging is that England is no longer dependent upon such old industries as coal-mining, textiles and shipbuilding, but is up in front among the leaders in ones which have the greatest prospects, such as aviation, telecommunications and banking. Sceptics may say these lack substance, that they provide few jobs, and require international markets as well as being too removed from the true necessities of life. All that is true; but what does it matter unless the English want to pull up the drawbridge and seek refuge in splendid isolation in an autarkic sulk? Far from sulking in a corner, the businessmen of England are as entrepreneurial, outward-looking, and venturesome as their forebears ever were. On any day of the week, Sundays included, several hundred of them can be found in the terminals of Heathrow, departing to the four corners of the earth. You will not find a comparable number of their competitors in the airports of Frankfurt, Tokyo or New York. Living near Reading, I use one of the local taxi firms; its main trade is ferrying businessmen between Reading and Heathrow, and it does this between ten and twenty times every day of the year except Christmas day. Its passengers come from just one medium-sized town, and every one of them is promoting Britain's business overseas. Half a century ago, the town's industries were based on seeds, biscuits and beer; the managers no doubt went beyond the bounds of Berkshire, but none would venture abroad. In this, as in so much else, the English are now little different from their distant forebears. The Anglo-Saxons were international traders, as archaeologists have found to their amazement when digging up bits and pieces that have come from thousands of miles away in the Middle East, Africa and Asia. The tradition goes back many centuries, and in the twenty-first century it is going to be as strong and deter-mined as it has ever been.

To win new business and prosper abroad, the British busi-nessman has proved that there is no necessity for his country to be in a trading *bloc* or any kind of economic union. Britain does more profitable trade with the United States than with France and Germany together, and moreover the trade is more reliable. Indeed, the European Community has been a severe disap-pointment in providing a worthwhile market for the UK. Until 1972 the value of exports from the UK to the six countries that were the founder-members of the Community tended to be higher than the value of the imports from the same six coun-tries, so that Britain used to make a net gain in trading with them. One reason for this was that labour costs in Britain were considerably lower, but the entry into the Common Market required food prices to rise dramatically, one of the factors that pushed British labour costs up by some 75 per cent. The other advantage was that Britain had higher industrial tariffs than the Common Market, and once those were eliminated, imports from the Continent became cheaper – hence the invasion of Renaults, Mercedes and Fiats which previously had to face a tariff duty of 17 per cent. Once we entered the European Community the favourable position was reversed, and in every year since then Britain has imported more from the rest of the EEC than she has exported to it. The balance of trade has become seriously adverse and now runs into billions of pounds. What this means in terms of jobs lost, it is difficult to say. In an earlier book, *Farming in the Clouds,* I calculated that not less than a million men and women in Britain have lost their employment as a result of this excess of imports over exports, and the estimate was never challenged.

One reason for this deterioration is that the English – more so than the Scots or Irish – are not chauvinistic in deciding what to buy. While other nations, and most notably the French, will query where the article comes from and weigh heavily in the balance the fact that it is made by their fellow countrymen, the English as a rule are indifferent to the country of origin. If the thing is what they want and the price is reasonable, it is theirs. Many an importer has prospered because the English lack this kind of prejudice; and foreign exporters tell how England is of all the large markets the easiest to penetrate. What this means, of course, is that whatever degree of independence the English chose to pursue, other countries would be rather silly if they were to erect barriers against English exporters; and none would be sillier than our neighbours on the Continent. To put it crudely, they would be cutting off their nose to spite their face, and doing so with a vengeance. Let it be added that England, even without Scotland, would still be a major oil producer, nearer to the Continent and more reliable than any other producer; and oil will remain a bargaining counter of inestimable value for several decades to come.

Any such talk of trade barriers presupposes that the World Trade Organisation had not been born, or despite its infancy lacks the teeth to bite. Its supra-national powers might be greater than some would wish, but none can doubt how far-reaching they are or their ability to prevent one country or trading *bloc* erecting barriers against another. The WTO is there; it stands guard over the global economy. If the English were to be so incapable of safeguarding their own interests in the world when others threatened some kind of trade war, the World Trade Organisation would be there to enter the fray. The very fact that this new supra-national organisation exists and is now firmly established should prevent any such threats, from the European Union or anywhere else.

In every century in the latter half of the second millennium there has been a profound and radical change in the governance of the British Isles. The departure of most of Ireland from the United Kingdom was such a change in the twentieth century, and we can be sure another upheaval is likely in the present century. As we thumb our way through the pages of an atlas, we realise that, in being subject to change, the British Isles are no different from any other part of the world; even the United States has not allowed its constitution to be set in stone. Nonetheless there has been a difference in how the English have made the fundamental changes. They have come about empirically, in a way that is consistent with their national culture; being empirical, they have for three centuries been at peace within their own land. Never mind the reason, their forebears have said, we want to make changes that work. Thus the details get sorted out, without reference to ideologues, still less on the advice of intellectuals in other countries. If we look back at what has happened to the evolution of England's governance it seems remarkable how comfortably the changes have come about, and how sensible the outcome has been. To claim some innate genius for this achievement would be going too far: more likely it is due to a willingness to change when change is necessary, but a reluctance to change in haste. Time will certainly be on the side of the English once it is clear, and it should be so now, that profound changes in governance are on the way.

To set out a blueprint at this stage about how a self-govern-ing English people will manage their affairs would therefore be contrary to how matters have evolved in the past. It would also be premature. We cannot tell when Scotland will secede; we can only speculate about the date when the nationalist population will decide the fate of Ulster. The future for Wales is equally uncertain, but there are at least forty nations smaller and with fewer national resources that prosper in a state of independence; and there is no practical reason why Wales could not add to their number. Her ties with England are stronger and longer, but they may not be enough to ensure a Union in perpetuity. Wales has much in common with New Zealand, where so many of her sons and daughters have emigrated to shape the landscape in the likeness of the land of their fathers, enabling Plaid Cymru to point to a paradigm.

Thus there is no "if" about the end of the United Kingdom, though the "when" must remain beyond our ken. There is no need to ponder the details about how the English will carry on their affairs. Events will force the pace, and the English, we can be sure, will find their way. To suppose they lack the ingenuity to devise the ways and means of doing so is to forget that some nine-tenths of Britain's governance has been originated by the English. For that reason the severance of the Union may be more of a constitutional trauma for the Scots than it will be for the English.

England's future outside the British Isles is a different issue, and it may be more difficult to resolve. Winston Churchill spoke of a place in three circles of friendship – the Commonwealth (which he firmly put first), the North Atlantic and Europe. Although the influence of each circle has changed, all three are certain to affect Britain's or England's role in the world. Politically, it has been policies of trade and defence that have created the circles, but for ordinary people, culture in one form or another cemented the links. Trade no longer binds the Commonwealth together politically, for entry into the EEC gave political control over trade to the institutions in Brussels. If they decreed, as they have done, that the British should no longer buy butter produced in Australia, then that is the law and it is a criminal offence to import her butter. Despite such barriers, trade in many other items carries on between our two countries. Millions of British people imbibe Australian wines in preference to others, and importers say is it partly due to a cultural prejudice. The General Agreement on Tariffs and Trade and now the World Trade Organisation have a greater effect upon trade policy than the European Union; and as the trade barriers disappear, so the political interference is pushed aside to allow ever more willing buyers and willing sellers to do business together to their mutual advantage irrespective of where they happen to be. GATT and WTO having diminished the impact of the Commonwealth circle, they are now having the same effect on the EU. On the other hand, they are bringing Britain closer to the US since Britain's economic cycle is similar to that of the US, and not to the EU's.

Defence policy has also brought Britain closer to the US. The US has been able to count on the support of Britain almost every time she has intervened outside her own territory, and usually the US president has initiated the actions only after consulting Britain's prime minister. On those occasions support has not been just moral (insofar as that has any meaning in this context) but active and immediate. Even when the US invaded Grenada, a Commonwealth country where the Queen was still head of state, the reaction of the British government to this flagrant outrage was muted. Much therefore has been said about a special relationship existing between the White House and Downing Street. Between Macmillan and Kennedy, Thatcher and Reagan, Blair and Clinton, the links have been of greater strength than at other times. The president felt little need, so it seemed, to listen to Wilson, Heath or Major, for reasons which may be understandable.

In the late 1960s a group of politicians from the United States, Canada and Britain was formed to promote the idea of a North Atlantic Free Trade Area. The objective was to bring the three countries together by ending tariff barriers that existed between them. For Canada and Britain, both enjoying Commonwealth preferences, the barriers between them were of little consequence. But the proposal would have brought the US and Canada and the US and Britain closer together. It fell on the deaf ears of Edward Heath, who was resolved that Britain should enter the EEC, whatever the terms might be, and the State Department looked forward to Britannia transmogrified as Uncle Sam's Trojan horse.

Since then another NAFTA, North American instead of North Atlantic, has been launched successfully, consisting of the US, Canada and Mexico. It was formed upon the same principles, that of a free trade area and not a customs union like the EU. (The difference is that a member of a free trade area is at liberty to have what trading arrangements it likes with third countries, whereas in a customs union that liberty is lost.) Ought Britain to join this NAFTA? Conrad Black, a man whose media interests in Canada, the US and Britain have given him immense influence in all three countries and can open any door in Washington and Ottawa as they can in London, insists that the option is there for the British people to choose. All that is necessary is for their politicians to agree and make the overture. If it is true that Britain has a choice to get closer to the rest of the EU or to the US and Canada, one assumes that it will apply to England too. As to whether it would suit the English, there is a simple test that might decide the issue. Do the English feel more at home in either the US or Canada than they do in, say, France or Germany, the two countries that form the dominant axis of the EU? Most of the English enjoy a holiday spent in France, if not in Germany, and part of the enjoyment is doing things differently. Many thousands have second homes in France, and perhaps a million or two would quite happily settle there for the rest of their lives, but whether it would be many more is questionable. When the

English want to emigrate, in overwhelming numbers they head for another part of the English-speaking world: the linguistic and cultural pull is hard to resist. The four elements of England's culture are, to a substantial degree, replicated across the Atlantic; and if culture, as defined in an earlier chapter, is the cement that binds a nation together, it must be obvious in which direction England should go, that is if her people feel it necessary to take either route. The fundamental difference between the two should not be overlooked. One requires an "ever-closer union" leading inexorably to some kind of megastate, while the other requires no more than the dismantling of trade barriers.

Even a free trade area will not be without its disadvantages, particularly when most of the powerful transnational corporations are American and not averse to flexing their muscles in Washington. There is an important example of what can happen in the case of genetically manipulated foods. Scientists employed by the US and UK governments have assured the public that there is no evidence that they are unsafe. This is not quite the same as saying they are certain that they are safe; and such toxicological evidence as is available has been supplied by the manufacturers themselves. And safety is not the only issue, for what we want to eat and drink is essentially a personal decision. Many have an ethical objection to playing God, others do not wish to endanger organic crops, and anyone who has seen how the multinational corporations have disrupted agriculture in the poorest countries may also have strongly held views. A government has no business to overrule the judgement of the people in these matters, or even their prejudices; and to do so is societally unnecessary as well as being a gross denial of an individual's freedom of choice. If GM foods are to be marketed, then most people would say they should be labelled accordingly so that an essentially personal decision can be made as people wish. That, though, is not to be the law on either side of the Atlantic. In NAFTA would the UK be allowed to have a different law? Environmentalists can think of other instances, such as the way the mighty chemical and pharmaceutical corporations succeed in having their own employees given jobs in the federal agencies which approve their products. In one case a scientist employed by Monsanto, which devised the hormone BST, transferred to the Federal Drugs Agency, where he was given responsibility for judging the very same product. In his report he concluded that no labelling of food treated with the drug was necessary. This denial of personal liberty is no small matter, but one advantage of negotiating a treaty would be that Britain would have a say in resolving such problems.

Whatever her future, England cannot help but be in Europe: it is a fact of geography and it is a fact of history that the English are European in every normal sense of the word. They share the Continent with at least a hundred other ethnic peoples, but large though it is, Europe is not as large as other continents and it has fewer natural resources than any of the others. Its distinguishing feature is that, despite its claim to be civilised, its people have the propensity to fight one another. Anyone disposed to thinking that there has been peace in the latter half of the twentieth century might remember that throughout most of that period there was warfare – cold warfare – in which billions of pounds, dollars and roubles were spent in devising ever more powerful nuclear weapons capable of destroying not just the whole of Europe but the whole world ten times over. In such a continent it might be wise for England to avoid becoming too entangled in its internecine affairs. Yet she cannot stand aside and pretend that what goes on in Europe is no business of hers. Even if she becomes the fifty-first state of the US, she would still remain a part of Europe. What then should be her relationship with the forty-odd other states of the Continent?

For a start we can look at three organisations that have an impressive record of achievement, much of it unknown to the public. They are the Council of Europe (not to be confused with the European Council, the title given to the twice-yearly summits of the political heads of state of the EU), the Economic Commission of Europe, and the Council on Security and Co-operation in Europe. Each of these three is open to all the states of Europe, although in the case of the Council of Europe, members are admitted only if they accept what they consider to be the rule of law and at least the rudiments of democracy. The CSCE has fifty-two member states, as the United States and Canada have joined on the ground that they are members of NATO; and a similar arrangement has been made for them to belong to the Economic Commission for Europe, which is an agency of the United Nations. There can thus be no doubt that England along with the other countries of the former UK would be admitted to membership of all three bodies.

The distinctive feature of the work of all three of them is that it is done internationally or inter-governmentally. They recognise the diversity of national interests among their members and make no attempt to coerce any one of them into agreeing to a measure that is against its interests. There are no rows, histrionics or horse trading, and of course that makes very dull copy for the media. As a result most people know very little about what these bodies are achieving.

It was Sir Winston Churchill, in a broadcast in 1943, who first conceived the idea that, once the war was over, the peoples of Europe should organise themselves for the purpose of international co-operation. Five years later he saw it come about when 700 delegates from 16 countries, with observers from 10 others, gathered in The Hague at the Congress of Europe. They resolved that there should be a European Assembly of Parliamentarians, and that a charter should be drawn up and a Court of Human Rights established. Its declared objective is European unity. The term, though, is misleading. There has been no attempt to merge all the countries of Europe into a single unity in the literal meaning of the word. Co-operation would be a more accurate word or a "coming together" to achieve a common purpose. The unity or "oneness" relates to the common interest, not to the countries themselves. The Council of Europe meets in Strasbourg. Both national governments and national parliaments are represented in it, and the Parliamentary Assembly of the Council can claim to be the first parliamentary institution of international status. It has, however, no pretensions to being a legislative body, nor can it "vote supply". Instead its role is deliberative and consultative. Unlike the European Parliament, which also sits in Strasbourg, it asserts no claim to supranational powers. Every country sends a delegation from its parliament to the Council's Assembly. This has plenary sessions but its principal work is undertaken by thirteen specialist committees which cover most governmental functions that can cross frontiers, except for defence and foreign affairs. One of these committees will examine an issue that is of common concern and then make recommendations to the Committee of Ministers. This is the Council's executive organ and, as its name suggests, consists of ministers from each member country concerned with that particular issue. The Committee may pass a resolution or agree to a convention. A resolution specifies the measures a member country should take to put into effect an agreed policy. A convention is an agreement that binds the member countries whose ministers have signed it, the best known example of the latter being the European Convention on Human Rights. This lays down certain fundamental freedoms and those members that have signed it have agreed to introduce laws giving effect to the Convention. This illustrates two of the Council's principles. First, no country is coerced by majority voting: there is no compulsion to take part in formulating a resolution or convention, and a country only joins in when its representatives believe it is in its interests to do so. Second, there is no attempt to usurp the power of the national parliaments, for any change in the law must be made by them.

The Economic Commission for Europe, is an agency of the United Nations. It was formed in 1947 to raise the "level of European economic activity" and to maintain and strengthen the economic relations of European countries. Ten years later it became the first international body to concern itself with environmental issues. It achieves its ends by passing resolutions about action to be taken by member countries. The Commission will only take up an issue if it believes there is a general agreement among the governments to achieve some co-operative action, and as a result there is seldom a wish to opt out by a member. Much of the Commission's business concerns quite mundane matters, but there have been some valuable achievements. For example, the standardisation of laws regulating inland transport, traffic signs and standards of driving throughout the Continent has been brought about by the work of the Economic Commission for Europe. Furthermore, this has been achieved without any country feeling imposed upon or aggrieved, for the Commission regards itself as the servant not the master of the member countries.

The third body is the Council on Security and Co-operation in Europe. It has three main concerns. The first is with security between the participating states. The second section is about co-operation in the fields of economics, science and technology, and the environment. The third section is about the protection of human rights. The Helsinki Final Act of 1975, which inaugurated the Council, was intended to govern relations between all the member countries subscribing to the Council, and it was meant to be politically binding, though the bombing of Yugoslavia showed that it was not.

None of these three bodies takes power away from the peoples of Europe. They are democratic in the sense that the EU is not and cannot be so long as the Treaty of Rome remains immutable. Were Canada, Norway, Iceland, Australia and New Zealand, which are unquestionably democratic, to form an international forum restricted to democratic states, they would be justified in denying membership to the EU or indeed to any of its member states, on the ground that they have eliminated from their system of government the basic tenets of democracy.

With that sobering thought in mind, what does England do about her membership of the EU? We are told we are locked in, and there is no procedure for withdrawal. Indeed the Treaty of Rome, as amended at Maastricht, goes further: once a new degree of integration has been agreed, there is no going back. That may be the wish of Britain's masters in Whitehall But once they give way to an English government and an English parliament the scene may shift dramatically. Sooner or later a majority will be elected to a new parliament which will call for the renegotiation of the Rome Treaty. There can then be no reason why an English government cannot assert itself, once elected by the English people on a mandate to restore their democracy.

To be "in Europe but not run by Europe", like all slogans, may lack precision. Nonetheless the general idea is plain enough for a constructive debate on what is crucial to Europe's future. It assumes that we will continue our participation in the Council of Europe, the Economic Commission for Europe and the Council on Security and Co-operation in Europe; moreover, it need not necessarily mean our leaving the EU itself. But it does mean that no matter what may be decreed by the institutions in Brussels, it will be an English government and an English parliament that can decide how the English people should be coerced by the two powers of government, legislation and taxation. Not until those two powers of coercion are fully restored to the legislators elected by and accountable directly to the English people will their country be a true democracy. Such a stance will be in Europe's interests, too. The EU can never be "Europe" until it includes some thirty or perhaps forty states. Is it conceivable that the abolition of the veto and the introduction of majority voting would not cause a widespread sense of injustice? To trample upon the interests of a minority may sometimes be justified; but when the minority may consist of one hundred or two hundred million people you have a prescription for trouble. There are two ways to strive for unity, the one adopted by the EU and the other by the Council of Europe. Perhaps it is a pity the two bodies cannot be merged together with the *modus operandi* of the latter.

Trade statistics may be tedious to read, misleading when selective and of passing validity. But at the end of a century which most people believe has brought Britain to her nemesis there is plenty of evidence to point to the contrary. Britain has at least the sixth largest economy in the world (and arguably the fourth or fifth) and only three – those of the USA, Germany and Japan – are significantly bigger. Germany's economy is on a plateau of minimal growth, with an intractably high level of unemployment and with many businessmen seeking to expand elsewhere, whilst Japan's economy in the 1990s has shown itself to be unstable. As for the United States, acting as the world's policeman is a costly business and Uncle Sam is becoming the poorer for it, just as the role beggared John Bull. It is adding billions of dollars to US indebtedness, and the day of reckoning will come. Britain has considerable advantages over each of those three major players. China may be poised to achieve great things, but it is not yet in the same league as Britain.

Since 1950 Britain's prosperity has grown steadily, making every house in the land, even the poorest, a more comfortable place than it used to be. No longer shouldering the White Man's Burden may be a contributory factor, for in the first half of the twentieth century any gain in trade with the Empire was out-weighed by the cost of defending and administrating a host of imperial outposts. But what must be certain is that membership of the EC has been a drain upon the nation's wealth. Throughout most of Britain's membership, she has been the second largest paymaster, her contributions to the EC budget adding up to over £200 billions at the current value of the pound. Although about half has been repaid, it has only been on schemes that the Commission wanted the money spent on, which is not necessarily how it would have been spent had the money remained in the hands of the Treasury.

With tedious repetition, we are told that 52 per cent of our trade is with our European partners and that $3^1/_2$ million jobs depend upon our EU membership. This includes the sale of our North Sea oil, an asset patently non-renewable which the experts say will be gone in the first half of the twenty-first century. Even if we take oil out, the figure is still misleading. Continual strikes and restrictive practices having brought the demise of London docks, once the largest in the world, Rotterdam has taken their place. Many of our exports go there to be shipped out again to their destination. To describe them as exports to the EC is scarcely honest, and when they are deducted the true figure of exports to the EC falls to 40 per cent. In terms of Britain's Gross Domestic Product, only 20 per cent of our trade is with the Eurozone. What is more this percentage is tending to fall, while our trade elsewhere is going up; and in the English-speaking world it is rising faster than anywhere else indeed the value is rising twice as fast.

Perhaps the most striking fact of all about Britain's economy is that she has a structural trade surplus with every continent on this planet – except one. The exception is Europe. Theoretically, at least, it might be to the advantage of the British people to trade only across the oceans, and this is something that becomes even more significant when we consider the future position of England outside the United Kingdom. It is not practical to separate out the trade figures for the different nations of the UK so as to arrive at the proportion due to England alone, but a not unreasonable estimate would be at least 80 per cent. Geography has made most of the industries and nearly all smaller business-es in the three other countries regionally orientated. The port of Glasgow is but a shadow of its past, and no airport has recovered the trade it has lost.

The dissolution of the United Kingdom, even partially, will lead to a few other difficulties to be resolved. There is the national debt. A nationalist government in Scotland will be in no mood to volunteer to accept its share, and one can hear it said that the national debt began with the founding of the Bank of England, and with that institution the debt can stay. From that historical truth a certain logic flows to which the English may have to succumb.

Then there is defence. If the justification for spending billions of pounds is to protect the nation from an external enemy, the Scots may say they will face no threat from abroad, and their money can then be spent on other things. While that will be an issue for the Scots to decide for themselves, it could be the time for the English to have a deep re-think about defence.

Having discarded the accoutrements befitting a great imperial power, the lesser forces of today's Britain may then be reduced still further. On the other hand, it has been England's tradition to take up the sword on behalf of the oppressed wherever they may be; and sometimes, as in South America, it has furthered her interests. Hence a balance may have to be struck, a decision that can be made only at the time.

These are practical questions and there is no reason why they cannot be satisfactorily settled. More fundamental, and perhaps harder to achieve, is the change in self-perception that the English have got to make. They are far too inclined to belittle themselves and their history, to accept guilt for every wrong their ancestors did but not to take pride in what they did well. Of course the English have, over the centuries, done many bad and cruel things, but then so have the people of every nation. The English seem almost to take pleasure in recalling that, in the eighteenth-century conflict with Scotland, 'Butcher' Cumberland brutally killed a number of Scots. The Scots, on the other hand, feel no guilt for the cattle raiders who killed any of the northern English who got in their way, or for the fact that under the old system of feuding clans far more Scots were butchered by fellow Scots than ever were killed by the English.

And of course the Scots are right. They are not responsible for the sins of their forebears, but they are the inheritors of a great tradition in which they rightly take pride.

If the English are to take a more balanced and open-minded view of their own past the first place to start is in the schools. Once again, we get nowhere by creating reversed images of past mistakes. Even if school textbooks a hundred years ago did present too rosy a picture of human progress and of the central part played by the enlightened British, that is not a reason to present them now as nothing more than oppressors or even to feel uneasy about teaching English history at all as a central part of the curriculum. The history of a culture is an important part of that culture and this is particularly true in a multi-ethnic society. A class of students drawn from many different parts of the world has more, not less, need to be taught the history of the society they have joined than one filled only be native children. Of course English history must be set in the context of world history but that does not mean that it is no more important than the history of the places from which the immigrant children have come. If I had decided to settle in Japan when my children were young I should have expected them to be taught Japanese history, with the history of England taking its place in a general history of the world.

Questions of this sort are important because, whatever England's constitutional future, it must surely be beyond all doubt that she is going to remain a country in which people of different colours and ethnic origins live. Whether these minorities add up to three, four or more millions, the number will represent a sizeable part of the population; and that too is another obvious truth which will never run away. The implication is so obvious that it sinks to banality, yet it must be stated because it is the crux of the argument. It is, of course, that the people who reside in England will not live at ease with one another unless they make a success of their multiracial society. The opposite of being at ease is being dis-eased, and as Leopold Kohr argued in his *Breakdown of Nations*,[1] a nation, like an individual, can be diseased. The symptoms are rising crime, rising divorce rates, pornography, deteriorating schools—in other words the same sort of list that the Muslim fundamentalists printed on the leaflet reproduced in an earlier chapter, which advertised their rally in Trafalgar Square. They blamed too much "freedom and democracy". Leopold Kohr denies that Western values bring about a nation's disease. He argues that it is a question of a nation's size. The smaller the population of a social unit, the easier it is to achieve social cohesion, and a consequent homogeneity. To take an extreme example, in a totally isolated village of 200 and 300 inhabitants, even selfish behaviour in a mild form soon becomes known and a good reputation is lost. Crime, being more readily solvable, is minimal; matrimonial troubles are less likely to end

[1] Leopold Kohr, *Breakdown of Nations*; Green Books, 2001.

in the divorce court; and no matter the ethnic mix, the inhabitants have a common interest in getting on well together, so that their differing values and beliefs tend to homogenise. Uproot those happy people and put them down in the streets of a large city and the decline begins. As people acquire the ability to escape from the company of others, so they can escape the consequences of their bad behaviour.

Two countries are not far from England across the sea, Iceland and Norway. Both have negligible crime rates and the other symptoms of a sick society are also virtually absent. In neither can the visitor detect the kind of mean poverty that is so visible in any of Britain's largest cities, as it is in large countries the world over. The evidence of social cohesion is overwhelming. There may be no extremes of wealth either, but the 300,000 Icelanders can afford to run an international airline, and charge fares lower than the other transatlantic carriers. They can afford it because such a healthy society hardly needs any governing. That their prime minister has a part-time job seems to say it all.

In Iceland what hope would there be for a trade union militant to organise a strike or a Trotskyist teacher to poison the minds of his pupils, or anarchists to go on the rampage through the streets? All three of those have been experienced in Britain. In every nation beyond a certain size, which allows the freedom to do so, people become agitators in one form or another. A better word may be *provocateur*. What really motivates them we do not know. The best of them are moved by frustration at an injustice not put right by constitutional means, but for too many of them it is the working out of private frustrations and inadequacies or the thrill of stirring a mob to disaffection and even violence. It could be the sense of power in a trade union or the school classroom;or a perverted intellect born of an embittered childhood becoming one of the more intelligent of society's drop-outs and misfits. Such people find no scope in small countries, largely because the gap between the government and the governed is itself small; and even a minor injustice can be readily known and rectified.

How different it is in any country with a population of 50 million. The kind of people described above abound in such a country. That they are not very apparent in Britain today is to some extent due to the paucity of injustices, to the curb of trade union power, and to the rooting-out of many of the far-Left teachers from the schools. Nevertheless, they exist, and despite their heads being below the parapet, they are at work. They can be found in universities, in the media and among social workers; and a Labour minister has told me he is convinced they have moved into the Civil Service. More importantly still, they are among the ethnic minorities as well as among poor whites who live in the same inner city areas.

No ground could be more fertile for the *provocateur* than a multi-ethnic, multicutural people, and the extremists on both sides have been quick to take advantage of it. It is an easy and obvious move to denounce the National Front and its successor parties. They are correctly spoken of as neo-Nazis, and what Hitler did in the 1930s is precisely what the *provocateurs* are attempting to do in the inner cities of England. They have been tailoring the message for the ears of the poor whites, and before the West Indians arrived they had turned their mischief upon the Jews, the bankers and the landlords in the East End. Inspired by Oswald Mosley, they called for a United Europe to prevent another European civil war (as I heard Mosley describe it at a meeting in Bethnal Green) so that "our working-class lads should never again fight their kindred". The neo-Nazis have always sought to gain their support from the labour ranks, competing with the Communists, which is essentially the reason why they have been and remain such bitter enemies.

The arrival of thousands of black people in certain districts, hitherto monopolized by poor whites, could not have been more fortunate for those neo-Nazis. To stir up fear was the obvious tactic, and without a doubt it worked; but it is significant that it only succeeded in poisoning a small minority. That ingredient of England's culture, toleration had much more effect.

Their Enemies the Communists, whether Stalinist, Maoist or Trotskyite, had their opportunity too and so had a mixed bag of other groups of the alienated and discontented. Among the immigrants they fomented hatred that was turned not just on the neo-Nazis, but extended to a generalised attack upon institutions of all kinds. In the case of the West Indians, most saw through the seductive overtures. Many had received a Christian upbringing and their beliefs would not let them accept what they heard from the class-cum-race warriors. When slighted by their hosts they shrugged their shoulders, and on Sunday mornings the black preacher exalted them to keep their self-respect as well as their faith. But many of their children found that message too difficult. Who were they? Born here, were they to call themselves British or like their parents did they feel they had ties with a faraway country unknown to them? It seemed that there was no country to which they fully belonged, and the hostility they encountered from the ignorant and bigoted increased their sense of alienation. Only someone who has experienced a crisis of identity can appreciate the difficulties that confront people in their position. They are in an emotional turmoil; anger is much more likely to be their response than cool reason; they are tugged in different directions, but seldom towards a happier view of the country in which they are living.

Nobody is more aware of the dangers ahead than West Indians (who would rather be so described than as Afro-Caribbean). They left the poverty of the countries where they were born to find a better life in Britain, and they found it. For the purpose of this book I have spoken to many of them. They are in responsible jobs, mainly in the public services, they own their own homes, almost all are churchgoers or attend one of the many chapels that now have a distinctly West Indian approach to Christianity, and they wish to remain here and be accepted (which makes them English). Their concern about the next generation is very great. One couple said, "We would like all the youngsters to be sent back by the government to Jamaica to see what their life would have been like if their parents or grandparents hadn't come here. Then they'd appreciate being in England."

There is nothing new in respectable hard-working parents having children who kick over the traces, take drugs and get into trouble, but for tens of thousands of young blacks it goes much further than that. The older generation may be made to feel ill at ease, and occasionally offended, but though that is highly regrettable it is something that is always liable to happen, especially to people whose skin colour serves as a badge to distinguish them from the hosts. It is notable, however, that older people do not feel alienated, aliens locked inside a country from which they cannot escape. This is the difference between the generations, and we cannot be surprised that as a result there are in the cities many thousands of the younger generations who feel frustrated and are therefore full of hate and too often violent.

These parents, or grandparents as they often are, see the dangers and realise how the behaviour of their children and grandchildren, now in their adulthood, will in the future prejudice the rest of the black people. Indeed, they have nothing but foreboding about the future – in, say, twenty years from now – when these young adults are middle-aged and have brought into the world another generation of hostile aliens. To them it is obvious that if their children reject the education offered to them, retreat into an emotional ghetto and despise those among them who aspire to an ordinary working life, too many of them are likely to end up unemployed and unemployable, easily tempted into crime, and dependent – their enemies would say parasitic – on the society they reject. Nothing could give a stronger impetus to anti-black prejudices.

Sadly none of these respectable parents and grandparents are raising the alarm loudly enough. Some of the clergy in the Pentecostal and other denominations which are principally composed of West Indians have spoken out individually, but that is not enough. What is important is that the excuses for feeling alienated should be dealt with firmly. The excuse that underlies the thinking and, therefore, the behaviour of the new generation of blacks is that England is a nasty racialist country whose people are all bigots and utterly prejudiced against the colour black. Who gives them this excuse? Of course the occasional bigot and the (more or less) organised far Right play their part, but sadly much blames attaches to some of the organisations that claim to be working for good relations. It is these organisations that have earned themselves the name of "the race relations industry" and their existence depends on finding racial bigots and making the most of their bigotry. Bigotry makes news and parts of the media have not been backward in giving publicity to the industry's press releases. A regrettable number of social workers, probation officers and teachers in their contacts with them lend support to this excuse. We can only guess what their motivation is, but it is known that the militant Left has become well represented in those three professions in the inner cities.

Forgetting the colour of one's skin may be difficult, but it will never get easier so long as the race relations industry and its allies persist in creating racial awareness, thus making people more conscious of the badge that they carry with them. If two people are having a quarrel it does no good at all to keep reminding one of them of all his real or imaginary grievances against the other. Any sane mediator would do just the opposite, trying to divert his mind away from them and getting them to see the good in his opponent. In the same way, the only route to good race relations is through making race less and less of an issue.

Those who stir up ill-feeling are not to be found merely among the militant Left. Lenin spoke of his "useful idiots". They are the less sophisticated people often wanting to do good and in the present context they have a vicarious guilty conscience about what was done in shipping slaves across the Atlantic and other misdeeds, real or imaginary, committed in the Empire. Now, given their assumptions, it is not unnatural that they wish to make amends. So far so good; but it is not good when they exacerbate racial awareness as, for instance, when they automatically agree with a black person who claims he has been prejudiced, even though there may well be an innocent interpretation of what was said or done. Nor should an embittered person, whether white or black, always be believed without ascertaining the whole story. These "useful idiots" tend to excite racial consciousness and so do much harm. Quite understandably they attack the neo-Nazis among the poor whites, but in doing so they grossly exaggerate their strength and influence, as any election proves. The extravagant claims they make about them serve only to evoke more fear among black people, which in turn induces even more consciousness about their colour and with it still further thoughts of prejudice and alienation.

Who, then, are Lenin's useful idiots of the twenty first century? The race relations industry has to be in the forefront, because it is setting the agenda. Every agency of the government is obliged to follow suit: everyone is meant to become imbued with this dangerous sense of guilt and to believe in the endemic hostility between races in Britain. There can be only one logical way to avoid this consciousness of race which in its growth is so divisive: it is to change the agenda.

In writing this book I heard many examples of these attempts to create racial consciousness where it did not exist before. On one occasion a youth club in the East End was visited by an official of the borough council who had every appearance of being on the militant Left. He asked to meet "the chair". When he heard of this, the chairman said he did not believe in "furniturism", which may not have got the conversation off to a good start. It continued as follows:

The official: *"I have come about the council's grant. I have to explain that its renewal depends upon the proportion of ethnic minorities in the club."*

The chairman: *"I simply don't know about them."*

The official: *"Then how many black members are recorded?"*

The chairman: *"That is something we would never think of recording. This is a club and open to any youngster who likes to join and accepts the rules. I don't care a damn about their colour, it has got nothing to do with their membership."*

The official: *"You can't receive a grant unless you record their ethnic origin, so that we can see from your books you are carrying out the council's policy."*

The chairman, disturbed by the line of conversation, called in the club's leader, a young man, black and of Jamaican origin.

Chairman: *"Do you know how many blacks or Asians are in the club?"*

Club leader: *"I have no idea."* A pause. *"I think there may be many more blacks than whites."*

Official: *"In that case you will be entitled to a renewal of the council's grant if you can prove it, but you must record the figures for inspection."*

Chairman: *"We will do no such thing. That is blatant racialism. You can keep the grant. I would rather find the money myself, and I will, rather than agree to this talk about race."*

The Club leader nodded his total support and the official went his way.

How does the multiculturalist answer this obvious question: Who has done more to create racial harmony in this corner of England? Is it the club leader in the numerous activities, social and sporting, that bring young people together, or is it the council official with his bribe to goad black youngsters to think of their racial difference?

It is not really a loaded question: it ought to be asked in those words because in the inner cities there are many other people like the chairman and club leader, often in voluntary organisations, and there are also many like the council official and his employers. The difference is that the influence that each can do is weighted against the former and in favour of the latter, and it has become national policy with taxpayers' money to make it weighted.

If all agencies of the state stopped raising the issue of race, the index of consciousness of racial difference would have a chance of falling several degrees. The vicious downward spiral – and it is indeed vicious – of this consciousness promoting fear which in turn adds to the consciousness which in turn creates still more fear, would then have a chance of being reversed. This alternative strategy would certainly not be to the advantage of the neo-Nazis or those who tend to share their views. They thrive on demonstrating racial differences and raising racial consciousness; and for them it is just as important as it is to the militant Left. The former, though, revel in the absurd decisions made by the race relations industry, as portrayed by the media. It is meat and drink to them, and another chance to raise the topic in a corner of the works canteen or down the road in the Pig and Whistle. And nothing fuels their filthy work more than a do-gooder who advocates positive discrimination.

Both these camps prosper in a country socially diseased, and racial tensions are a symptom of the disease. They will be eradicated only when England is able to establish herself as a single coherent society with a high degree of independence – and that means genuine independence not just within Europe and the world at large but also within Britain itself. Unfortunately just as the English have become over-diffident about their place in the world at large, they are reluctant to assert their claim to an identity of their own even within Britain. This can be seen clearly enough in the BBC. Once a very English institution, its ethos has transformed it into something very different. Neither "English" nor "England" are words used in its programmes unless it is totally impossible to use another, lest a Scot residing somewhere south of the Border takes umbrage. With severance of the Union the BBC will face a dilemma. For the people of England it will be of inestimable benefit to have this most powerful branch of the media forced to call itself English. Much good could follow: the culture (in the primary sense of the word) of England will at last have a proper opportunity to be explored, and if the Corporation's producers demurred, an English government would have the power to adjust its budget. And the more the English can know about the culture they have inherited, the more a sense of English identity will be achieved. This, of course, will not only enhance a feeling of homogeneity and therefore national unity, but also – and most important – give those of immigrant origin a reason to appreciate Englishness and absorb the values of their adopted country. That in its turn will advance the cause of assimilation.

To think of a group of people which has done more to belittle Englishness than the BBC policy-makers would be quite difficult enough; because it has been done so surreptitiously their efforts have too often gone undetected. Their suppression of the words "England" and "English" gives us a hint; confirmation is afforded when one recalls how often anything pertaining to the country is demeaned, their annual sneer at St George's Day being evidence enough. It is true that most of the English do not even know the date of St George's day, but that in itself has some significance. The other members of the UK celebrate their national days and the media would not dream of belittling them.

The English may shrug their shoulders and speak of this as adult, indicating a nation's maturity or demonstrating the self-confidence of a people with no need to assert themselves. Up to a point that is true, and for the intellectually minded it may be a satisfactory reaction. But some ninety per cent of the English are of a different mould. Their innate patriotism and the fact that they have a need for some degree of pride in their country – an expansion of their own self-esteem, which in their ordinary lives may be lacking – will impel them to look for a substitute. That substitute has been found in sport, notably football and to an extent cricket. The drunken louts, with their red, white and blue, who surge down the streets of foreign cities are a vivid part of the substitute. That eleven men can run around kicking a ball more adroitly than eleven men from another country may be a matter of great moment, but it should be conceivable to think of other reasons to enhance a nation's self-worth, and so stir the embers of true and unaggressive patriotism.

Too many people now speak of patriotism as if it was a vice, or at least led inevitably to jingoism and xenophobia. As was pointed out earlier, this is untrue, and indeed it is the very reverse of the truth. The Nazis did not come to power in a Germany that was confident, united and assured of its place in the world. They could only have gained their malignant hold over a nation that was defeated, fragmented and self-distrustful.

The English today are not a defeated people. True, they came close to economic defeat in the decades that followed the Second World War, but they have put that behind them and are now a successful people. They are, however, far too self-distrustful and, partly because of that, they are reluctant to take the steps that will save them from fragmentation. Indeed they have been reluctant even to see that as a danger, preferring to take refuge in talk of a "multi-cultural society". The phrase is far too glib to describe the alienation of many young people in the great cities or of the immigrants who form themselves into closed, self-protective, inward-looking communities. A society is, by its nature, a people united by a common culture: a collection of mutually mistrustful sub-groups is not a society at all.

The English are, and from the beginning always have been a nation of immigrants, a prime example throughout their history of a multi-racial society. But it will not continue successfully unless the English face the fact that multi-racialism can thrive only within the context of a common culture to which all its people feel they belong and which, in all important respects, they accept. To make that possible we all need first of all to be informed, the indigenous people about their own culture, the newcomers about the culture they are joining. And no one need be uneasy at the thought that, when people come to England, the culture they join is English It is a culture with a great past and it can have a great future. In the world today there is an honourable and important place for England.